Before You Know... He Knows

Enjoying a Life-Giving Relationship with Christ
by David E. Beroth

Live God's best for you!

Dave Beroth

John 10:10

des moines first assembly

2725 merle hay rd • des moines, ia 50310
515-279-9766 • www.desmoinesfirst.org

Before You Know . . . He Knows
Enjoying a Life-Giving Relationship With Christ
by David E. Beroth

Printed in the United States of America
ISBN 978-0-615-20698-1
© 2008, First Assembly of God Church, Des Moines, IA

All rights reserved. No part of this publication may be reproduced, stored in a retrieval system or transmitted in any form or by any means — electronic, mechanical, photocopying, recording or otherwise — without prior written permission.

For information:
First Assembly of God, 2725 Merle Hay Rd, Des Moines, IA 50310

Dedication

To Elli, my wife, God's greatest gift,
whose prayers, words, commitment and life
have taught me and continue to teach me
much that is in this book.

To my twin boys, Levi and Matthew,
who inspire me to become a better me.

To Kelli, my first daughter-in-law, Levi's wife, the
mother of Lukis, and the fun in our family.

To my first grandson, Lukis, who fills my life
with much joy and laughter.

Acknowledgements

This book is a team effort! No one writes a book alone. Books are products of teams and reflect the influence of friends, colleagues, and partners. From the first word to the last, I have been conscious of my friends watching my back, encouraging, supporting and believing in me.

Before I thank the team who helped produce this book, I want to thank my first ministry assistant. Thank you, Deanne, for your encouragement to write, not just from my head, but also from my heart.

I realize that you would not be reading this book without the very capable team I now have.

My executive assistant, Diana Koontz — You make my daily life doable. I am indebted to you as you selflessly serve me and First Assembly in so many ways. Thank you for proofing, reproofing and preparing this project for the refining process. Your ministry makes mine possible.

Kathy Koontz — You redefine "above and beyond." Thank you for pulling out that which was not needed and refining what was good.

Brittney Roorda — Thank you for your gift of creativity in the layout and design and acting as a liaison with Purcell for the final product.

The Team at Des Moines First Assembly — I am so grateful for you! You read chapters before they were complete and shared insights as they were in the working stages. Thank you for your work behind the scenes on a daily basis, offering your skills as worship to God, helping First Assembly fulfill the Great Commission as a healthy, visible, and growing community of Christ-followers.

My church family — I want to express my heartfelt thanks to the wonderful congregation of believers God has allowed me the joy of leading. I continue to be inspired by your desire to know Jesus more completely and love him more deeply. You are simply the best!

Tom Purcell and Purcell Printing — Thank you for the ideas, the samples, and for producing a quality product.

Justin Bopp — Thank you for your creative skill and the gift of your photo for the cover.

Contents

Introduction	8
1. He Knows	10
2. Come To Me	24
3. Ask Me	50
4. Remain In Me	70
5. Depend On Me	104
6. The Greatest News of All Time	138
Appendix	146
Endnotes	158

Introduction

All of us enjoy receiving invitations — to a meal, a wedding, or a concert. Usually, when the invitation is printed on a little card, there are cryptic letters written at the bottom: RSVP. These letters are an abbreviation of a French request to reply to the invitation. Most of us know what these letters mean, but, unfortunately, not everyone does.

A couple found political asylum in this country during the Second World War. They came from Eastern Europe, and they were not well versed in American culture. One day, they received an invitation to a wedding, and at the bottom of the invitation were those cryptic letters: RSVP. In his thick, Eastern European accent, the husband said, "Vife, vat does it mean, RSVP?" They thought for a while, until inspiration dawned, and the husband said, "Vife, I know vat it means: Remember Send Vedding Presents."

This sweet couple made a mistake by imagining that the message was a demand, when, in reality, it was an invitation. Unfortunately, there are many people who make the same mistake when giving their lives to God. They think it is a demand, when, in reality, it is an offer — a free invitation.

In even the most invigorated life, there comes the day when our noble career in teaching means just one more lecture; our interesting job in sales, just one more airport; our dedication to the joys of motherhood, just one more sibling squabble. The daily routine gets old. That is why exhaustion is one of the most prominent social problems of our time.

Sometimes, even religion is a burden. Going to church, reading the Bible, and family devotions can become tiresome, no more than a duty and a habit that is continued by inertia rather than commitment. This was probably the burden of which Jesus was speaking when He lamented how the religious leaders placed heavy burdens on people's backs and would not lift a finger to remove them (Matthew 23:4). The blessing of religion can become a burden when religion is reduced to should, ought, and must — a series of solemn commands. There are those who spend their whole lives getting over the damage done by "religion." Jesus sought to unburden people from oppressive religion. "Come to me, all of you who are weary and carry heavy burdens, and I will give you rest" (Matthew 11:28, NLT).

I am a firm believer that we all need rest, so it is time to RSVP. I hope you enjoy this book, which is all about an invitation, not a demand. So come as you are.

Before You Know . . . He Knows

1 He Knows

13 *The LORD is like a father to his children, tender and compassionate to those who fear him.* 14 *For he understands how weak we are; he knows we are only dust.* 15 *Our days on earth are like grass; like wildflowers, we bloom and die.* 16 *The wind blows, and we are gone — as though we had never been here.* 17 *But the love of the LORD remains forever with those who fear him. His salvation extends to the children's children*
Psalm 103:13-17 (NLT)

Many are the plans in a man's heart, but it is the LORD's purpose that prevails.
Proverbs 19:21 (NIV)

He Knows

Providence: a. divine guidance or care b. God conceived as the power sustaining and guiding human destiny.

All that I know of tomorrow is that Providence will rise before the sun.
Jean Baptiste Lacordaire

There is special providence in the fall of a sparrow.
William Shakespeare

Finish what you started in me, God. Your love is eternal — don't quit on me now.
King David, Psalm 138:8 (MSG)

In the movie *Next*, Cris Johnson, a Las Vegas magician (played by Nicholas Cage), reads minds, or so he leads everyone to believe. What he really does is see two minutes into his future and change events to materialize in a more positive way.

Cris' dexterity with the portals of time has not gone completely unnoticed. The club security guards are watching through their all-seeing casino floor cameras, eager to decipher his knack for consistently beating the odds. When a nuclear threat is discovered on American soil, the FBI discovers his gift and wants him to help track down the terrorists.

The plot clots, however, as Cris has plans of his own. At one point, to his surprise, he sees a lot further than two minutes and it involves more than just his future. Soon he's forced to choose between saving the world . . . or saving himself.

What would it be like to have the ability to see into your future? I cannot even imagine the responsibility. The decisions and choices you would have to contend with could be overwhelming. Though it might be appealing at first, if you really think about it, you might not want to see into your future for more reasons than mentioned. What happens when all the possibilities and excitement of what has yet to come consume you? You could miss or lose the significance of the now moment.

John Maxwell brings this idea to bear in his book, *Today Matters*. By focusing on proper involvement in the immediate, we are better equipped for the impending. In other words, the way you live your life today is preparing you for your tomorrow. In fact, "the only adequate preparation for tomorrow is the right use of today."[1]

On June 3, 2007, the First Assembly community voted me to be their lead pastor. I did not see that coming. Yet God did. In fact, He knew this would be a reality on June 4, 2006, the day our former senior pastor of 21 years resigned. Even as I was daily fulfilling my responsibilities as a pastor in Montana during the '90s, God was at work preparing me for my future role. While you cannot see into your future, you can prepare for it by trusting God today.

Biblically, we refer to this as the Sovereignty of God. As a meaningful and personally-impacting belief, we as Christ-followers affirm that God has not merely created the universe, together with all its properties and powers, and that He is preserving all that He has created, but that as a holy, benevolent, wise, and omnipotent being, He also exercises sovereign control over it. This sovereign control is called providence.

Charles Hodge writes, "This sovereignty of God is the ground of peace and confidence to all his people. They rejoice that the Lord God Omnipotent reigneth; that neither necessity, nor chance, nor the folly of man, nor the malice of Satan controls the sequence of events and all their issues."[2]

Illustrative encounters of God's special care pervade the Gospels as real life encounters Jesus. We take comfort and confidence in the truth that He is involved in the circumstances of our lives. One particular event stands out to me. Maybe it is familiar to you as well.

> *5 Jesus soon saw a great crowd of people climbing the hill, looking for him. Turning to*

Philip, he asked, "Philip, where can we buy bread to feed all these people?" 6 He was testing Philip, for he already knew what he was going to do (John 6:5-6, NLT).

John recorded from his perspective the only miracle that is in all four Gospels: the feeding of the five thousand (Matthew 14:13-21; Mark 6:32-44; Luke 9:10-17). This miracle has a rich tapestry of fundamental themes that weave through the life of Christ: Jesus' compassionate care for seekers, His complete control over creation, and the ability to make provision for life.

This miracle of provision indicates how Jesus meets our needs. But don't miss the obvious. He does so because of His matchless care. Maybe the other Gospel writers did not include it because it was so obvious. John, however, is unmistakable in his perception. "He was testing Philip, for he already knew what he was going to do" (vs. 6).

More than once, Jesus demonstrated unmatched awareness and responsiveness. "Immediately Jesus knew in his spirit that this was what they were thinking in their hearts, and he said to them, 'Why are you thinking these things?'" (Mark 2:8, NIV).

Jesus also surprised His companions on several occasions as He in essence spoke directly to their hearts, thus revealing He has a ministry that can meet our most fundamental needs.

> *7 They decided he was saying this because they hadn't brought any bread. 8 Jesus knew what they were thinking, so he said, "You have so little faith! Why are you worried about having no food? 9 Won't you ever understand? Don't you remember the five thousand I fed with five loaves, and the baskets of food that were left over?"* (Matthew 16:7-11, NLT).

The disciples, though not entirely surprising, lacked understanding for the way Jesus was going to provide for the hungry seekers. The disciples needed to see that they could accomplish things they never dreamed of doing through their association with Jesus. Only the limit of their vision would prevent them from moving confidently into their future.

"I could never do that" might be one of the greatest killers of your future. This phrase usually breaks the surface because of practical concerns, fear, or not enough information regarding the future outcome. In the process, dreams dissolve and forward movement turns into a frustrated wiggle.

Robert Redford wrote and directed a movie about a family in Montana whose lives in some way had been affected by a river that ran through their locale. The movie was given an appropriate title, *A River Runs Through It*. It is the story of the MacLean family, who lived in Montana early in the twentieth century. The father of the family was a Presbyterian minister; he was stern but loving. His wife was supportive and nurturing. They had two sons, Norman, the older son who tells the story, and Paul, the younger son.

The real protagonist in the story is the river that runs through Montana. The river becomes the focal point of their family life and the catalyst for everything significant that takes place in their individual lives. It was while walking along the banks of that river on Sunday afternoons that the father forges a relationship with his young boys — turning over rocks, teaching them about the world, about life and about God who made it all. It was to the river that the boys ran after their studies were finished, and sibling rivalry and brotherly affection flourished as they fished for trout together on that beautiful stream.

When it came time for these adolescent boys to prove their moxie, they took a death-defying ride down the rapids in a stolen boat. It was on the river that young Paul made a name for himself as the finest fly fisherman in the territory. When Norman came back from college, searching for himself and his roots, it was to the river that he went to fish with his brother.

The MacLean family knew of failure, success, laughter, fighting, change and disappointment, but always the river was there. Montana, for them, would have been just a wilderness; their home, four walls and a roof; their individual lives, just sound and fury — if not for the river running through it all.

I suggest that there is a river running through the lives of Christ-followers and that river is the providence of God. The ancient writer of Proverbs penned, "You can make many plans, but the LORD's purpose will prevail" (Proverbs 19:21, NLT). The intentionality of God must be our mainstay if we are to enjoy forward movement in life. The alternative is that our lives will be no more than a wilderness of activity if not for the purpose of God.

Friend, whatever has happened to you in the past, or whatever your present circumstances may be, whatever the future might hold, know this: A river runs through it, and that river is called the providence of God.

18   Before You Know . . . He Knows

Have you taken to heart that your connection with Christ changes the equation of what is possible? Jesus is the source of spiritual direction and provision. *Before you know . . . He knows!*

Our lives are not the result of chance. We didn't come from nothingness. To think otherwise would strip human life of any meaning. Unfortunately, this was the view of playwright Samuel Becket, who put forth a play entitled, *Breath*. The curtain opened to a bare stage littered with nothing but garbage — no actors, no dialogue. The script was nothing but a soundtrack, only 30 seconds in length, beginning with a baby's cry and ending with an old man's dying gasp.

The curtain closed. Becket's point is clear: Life is absurd, man is meaningless, and existence is pointless.

In contrast, the worldview of the Bible is profound. If we are made by a designer, then we are not here by chance. Life is not a series of random developments. We were created for a reason. There is intentionality about each and every one of us. We are not accidents. We were meant to be.

In 1858, a Sunday School teacher, Mr. Kimball, influenced a Boston shoe clerk to surrender his life to Jesus Christ. The clerk was Dwight L. Moody, who became an evangelist. In 1879, while preaching in England, the heart of a pastor named F.B. Meyer was awakened to a new passion. Eventually this passion led him to an American college campus to preach. Under his preaching, a student by the name of Wilbur Chapman gave his life to Christ. Chapman engaged in YMCA work and employed a former baseball player named Billy Sunday to do evangelistic work. Billy Sunday held a revival in Charlotte, North Carolina. The revival stirred the hearts of many, resulting in some thirty businessmen wanting to devote a day of prayer for Charlotte.

In May of 1934, a farmer loaned the businessmen some land to use for their prayer meeting. The leader of these businessmen, Vernon Patterson, prayed that, "out of Charlotte, the Lord would raise up someone to preach the gospel to the ends of the earth." The businessmen called for another evangelistic meeting with preacher Mordecai Ham, a fiery Southern evangelist who shattered the complacency of church-going Charlotte. The farmer who loaned his land for the prayer meeting was Franklin Graham. Because of his involvement, Graham's son, Billy, became a Christ-follower while listening to Mordecai Ham preach.

"Wow! What a coincidence," some might

say. "Who would have ever dreamed or imagined that because a Sunday School teacher told a young man about Jesus, it would turn out the likes of Billy Graham. Now is that luck or what? If that isn't fate I don't know what is!" What else could it be? Answer: Providence. Who would have ever imagined or dreamed a Sunday School teacher leading a young man to Christ would have such an impact, both now and eternally? The answer is God.

How about your life? Are there a series of events in your life that may appear to be luck or chance? That is exactly what the world would want us to believe about such events in our lives. "It's all just luck," they say. Others would have us believe such things as:

FATALISM: the view that all things are determined by an untouchable law of cause and effect. In other words, fate.

DEISM: the idea that God created the world, but then withdrew from the day-to-day caring of it.

DUALISM: the view that two opposing forces in the universe are locked in a struggle with each other for control.

God has something different to say about the everyday events and circumstances in which we find ourselves. It's called God's providential care. Do you know how many times the word *coincidence* (or any other word like it) is used is the Bible? Zero. Not one event in all of Scripture is ever spoken of as having been coincidental.

In 1937, Walt Disney released the first full-length animated movie, *Snow White and the Seven Dwarfs*. Producing an animated movie was a gargantuan task. Disney artists drew over one million pictures. Each picture flashed onto the screen for a mere one-twenty-fourth of a second.

Today, as we watch the movie at regular speed, it seems so simple. We are not aware of all that went into the production. Our lives are similar to the making of that movie. God put infinite thought, skill, and attention into every detail. Yet as our lives unfold at "regular speed," we are not aware of how much God's providence fills every single second.

With providence meaning to see and know in advance, we can conclude that God sees the impact our lives will make. The essence of a providential life is catching a vision not only for what God is doing in the world, but for what he wants to do through you! The people who have the greatest impact for Christ are those with the clearest sense of God's purpose and plan for their lives.

The book you hold in your hands is an

invitation to walk bravely into your future as you accept Jesus' invitation to "Come to me," "Ask me," "Remain in me," and "Depend on me." Follow Jesus into His desired future for you. That's where I'm headed. Will you join me?

He Knows 23

Before You Know . . . He Knows

2 Come To Me

28 Then Jesus said, "Come to me, all of you who are weary and carry heavy burdens, and I will give you rest. 29 Take my yoke upon you. Let me teach you, because I am humble and gentle, and you will find rest for your souls. 30 For my yoke fits perfectly, and the burden I give you is light."

Matthew 11:28-30 (NLT)

Come To Me

Rest: relief from anything distressing, to get ease and refreshment, to become still, to rely.

. . . you have made us for yourself, and our heart is restless until it rests in you.
Augustine, *Confessions, Book 1*, p. 43.

My grandson is too young to know this, but when his mom and dad bring him over, I have this routine. I drop everything I am doing and wait at the door for his arrival. As they approach the door, he can see me in the window aside the front door. When our eyes meet, he smiles, knowing that he is at "Papa's" house. I think the smile on my face is bigger.

We know that Jesus is the door to salvation, but we often forget that He is the door to LIFE. We trust Jesus to save our soul, but many of us are afraid to trust Him for our joy. We try to be happy without Him. We try to be successful without Him. We try to make our own rules and play the game our way, and as a result, we end up carrying a burden too great to bear.

The New Testament teaches that Jesus is the focus of all creation, the very center of the universe. And He says to us, "Come to me . . . make me the center of your life, and I will give you rest."

There is a particular story in the Gospel of Luke of a father who waits for the return of his errant son. Luke gives some indication that the father waits and looks down the road for the boy. At a certain point, while still a long way from home, the boy realizes his folly. He has made a major mistake in leaving his father's house. Wrong decisions usually lead to more wrong decisions, creating even greater wrong. Tired and weary of this downward cycle, he weighs the difference between living in the far country and living at home under his father's roof. He decides to go home to his father and say, "Father, I have sinned against both heaven and you." True. "I am no longer worthy of being called your son." Probably true. "Please take me on as a hired man." The only alternative in his mind (Luke 15:17-19, NLT).

He starts home on his own. Scripture says his father sees him when he is yet a long way off. What is going to happen? The father runs down the road to meet his son. He throws his arms around him. He kisses him. The boy begins his rehearsed speech. "Father, I have sinned against both heaven and you." True. Then the father interrupts him in the middle of his speech. He isn't interested in this groveling statement, "Take me on as a hired man. Turn me into nothing. I'm a worm. Step on me." The father has no intentions of doing that. He says, "Listen. Get a robe. Put a robe on the boy. Put a robe on the boy! Get a ring! There's no ring on his finger! Go out and get that calf we've fattened and kill it — let's have a party, because my boy is home" (Luke 15:21-24, NLT).

That is the most remarkable idea. It is more than a story about a son who misused the family fortune. It is more than a story about the repentance of a wayward son who decided to return home. It is more than a story about the jealous elder son who grudgingly stayed home to help the father manage the family farm. It is much more than all of that.

It is about the amazing active love of this father. "And while he was still a long distance away, his father saw him coming. Filled with love and compassion, he ran to his son, embraced him, and kissed him" (Luke 15:20, NLT).

I am awestruck by two realities of this father's love. As Luke recaps Jesus' story, he sketches a portrait of a father who had been looking for his son to return and noticed him the very moment he came into sight. When he saw him, though beneath the dignity of his status, he ran to his boy, held him, and kissed him.

Astonishing, isn't it? He ran toward him, held him, and kissed him. The word that Luke uses to describe the kiss reveals the father kissed him much, again and again.

What is the most extravagant expression of love you have received? Honest consideration to this question might have helped the Pharisees process this story. Jesus invested time in relating this story because they posed a question as to why He hung around sinners.

Pharisees were the ones you would have expected to embrace the ministry of Jesus. They were Bible believers, they looked expectantly for the coming Messiah, and they were strict in their obedience to the rules and requirements of the Old Testament. Strangely, this was the source of their conflict with Jesus. You see, He didn't keep all the rules the way they thought He should.

The problem with the Pharisees was that they were religious, but they were not spiritual. By its very nature, this kind of religion can only lead to guilt or pride. If you have a strict set of standards and can stick to those rules, then you have reason to be proud. If, however, you find yourself unable to live up to your strict standards, then you have reason to feel guilty. Both can lead to an exhausting existence.

Fortunately, Jesus' invitation, "Come to me, all you who are weary and burdened, and I will give you rest," can reposition us from under the weight of religion and bring us to the place where we can enjoy the advantages of a life-giving relationship. He wants us to recognize that Christianity is not following a bunch of do's and don'ts; it is living out a relationship with a Father who runs toward us, embraces us and kisses us.

How might we enjoy the advantages of a life-giving relationship with Christ? I would like to suggest two practices to employ.

The first practice is to accept His invitation daily.

You have most likely heard the old adage, "sounds too good to be true."

Robert Kirkpatrick had some good news and some bad news. The good news: He had been extended a written invitation to a dinner with President Bush in Washington, D.C. The invite and letter were signed by Vice President Cheney himself. It is not every day you receive an invitation like that. On the other hand, it was a fundraising dinner and the cost would be $2,500 per plate. You might think that was the bad news. Not in this case.

The bad news: When Kirkpatrick received the invitation in 2001, he was just beginning a three-year stint at the Belmont Correctional Institution in eastern

Ohio. He was serving time for drug possession and attempted escape. In the day of computer-generated mailing lists, such mistakes happen all the time.

Kirkpatrick was philosophical about the invitation. He told reporters, "I'm going to tell him that I'd be happy to attend, but he's going to have to pull some strings to get me there."[1]

Unless we appreciate who is making the offer and their ability to make good on the offer, we are not likely to give a second's notice to their invitation. Jesus' invitation is not a mistake, and His promise to receive us is reliable. In fact, life becomes more than bearable when the future holds promise. We can accept His invitation without hesitation and look forward with confidence that He will fulfill His promise.

Two vivid images come to mind when I think of promises. One is the picture of Joe Namath, the Jets' rogue quarterback, sitting poolside in Miami prior to the 1969 Super Bowl and promising (actually guaranteeing!) that the upstart New York Jets would defeat the heavily favored Baltimore Colts — a promise he kept several days later to the shock of the sporting world. Namath calmly directed the Jets on four scoring drives, completing 17 of 28 passes for 206 yards, and was voted the MVP in the victory over the stunned Colts. The Jets were the first AFL team to win the Super Bowl.

The other image is from the incident on October 18, 1970. Twenty-one months after their Super Bowl meeting, Namath suffered a fractured right wrist and threw a career-worst six interceptions in the Jets' 29-22 loss to the Colts.[2]

The simple reality is that a promise is only as good as the willingness and the ability of a person to follow through with it. Namath was only lucky on his boastful and swaggering guarantee regarding Super Bowl III. He could not come through on that promise every time he met the Colts.

What a comfort to know that when Jesus makes a promise, He not only has the willingness to make the promise but also the eternal integrity and ability to keep it. Note how Jesus describes Himself. "I am humble and gentle." However, do not make the mistake and assume that humble and gentle is weak. We find one of the many names ascribed to Jesus in Revelation 19:11 (NLT):

> 11 *Then I saw heaven opened, and a white horse was standing there. And the one sitting on the horse was named Faithful and True.*

In this particular verse, Jesus is identified as the rider of the white horse, and His name is "Faithful and True." What an impressive name! What joy it should bring to your heart to realize that Jesus is always truthful in what He says, and He is always faithful in bringing it to pass. His good name should assure you that He will fulfill His promises to you.

When Levi and Matthew, our twin boys, were a bit more than toddlers, they would greet me on many occasions by jumping from the stairs as I rounded the hallway. The routine sounded something like this, "Hey Dad! Catch me!" I would look up to either Levi or Matt joyfully jumping from the top of the stairs straight at me. An instant circus act would ensue; I would catch them and fall to the ground in a heap. The first time this happened, for a moment after I caught Levi, I could hardly talk because of the shock. Never did I scold them, though I did mention the danger of the activity for their mom's sake. I thought it was an incredible display of trust. Their whole assurance was based on the fact that I would catch them. They jumped, because as their dad, I could be trusted.

Of the many profound and significant promises Jesus made, few have more day-to-day potential impact on our lifestyles than the promise of rest. "Come to me, all you who are weary and burdened, and I will give you rest." Jesus' words, "Come to me," could be translated as, "Jump, I will catch you!"

Let me give you a practical suggestion on jumping skills. Some years ago, I decided to begin my day with two simple habits, each of which has made a big difference in the whole flow of my day. First, when I wake up, I think about the goodness of God and run through a list of things for which I am grateful. When I adopted this habit, I was not a morning person. Thus, even more reason to start my day on a positive note. I have noticed through the years that this practice has helped me examine my attitudes before they become hazardous, and it helps me keep good tabs on what is really happening in my heart and mind. This simple habit has become a mental demonstration of how I want to live my life — grateful, positive, and God first.

Second, after my feet hit the floor and I take care of morning hygiene, I head for my Bible. I spend a few minutes reading a passage that I've chosen for that season of time and I meditate on it. Later in my schedule, I have time set aside for more concentrated study, but these few morning moments help order my life for the day.

These two simple habits are my way of accepting Christ's invitation to come to Him. Learn to jump — it's fun.

The second practice is to take time to grow your soul.

When we are welcomed into adulthood, it seems like we are handed a to-do list with a deadline of yesterday. We begin our climb up the mountains of responsibilities and over the hills of obligations. We muddle on through the valley of weariness, while the list of chores we were given yesterday has grown today. Our focus is on accomplishing the tasks rather than on the quality of our performance. We live in a very tense, uptight and fast-paced world.

Many people suffer from what John Ortberg calls "hurried sickness" in his book, *The Life You've Always Wanted*. He reminds us of the world of the Red Queen in *Alice in Wonderland*. " . . . it takes all the running you can do to keep in the same place. If you want to get somewhere else, you must run at least twice as fast as that!"[3]

Where is somewhere else? And why is it so important that we get there? Maybe we are just caught in the updraft of our culture.

It reminds me of an incident of an older man

on a moped who drives up alongside a younger man with a brand new Ferrari 550. The old man looks over at the sleek, shiny car and asks, "What kind of car ya' got there?" The young man replies, "A Ferrari 550. It cost half a million dollars!" "That's a lot of money," says the old man. "Why does it cost so much?" "Because this car can do up to 320 miles an hour!" states the young dude proudly. The moped driver asks, "Mind if I take a look inside?" "No problem," replies the owner.

The old gentleman pokes his head in the window and looks around. Then sitting back on his moped, he says, "That's a pretty nice car, all right . . . but I'll stick with my moped!" Just then, the light changes, and the guy decides to show the old man just what his car can do. He floors it, and within 30 seconds, the speedometer reads 160 mph. Suddenly, he notices a dot in his rearview mirror. It seems to be getting closer! He slows down to see what it could be, and suddenly, whhhoooossshhh! Something whips by him, going much faster!!!

"What on earth could be going faster than my Ferrari?!" the young man asks himself. He floors the accelerator and takes the Ferrari up to 250 mph. Then, up ahead of him, he sees the old man on the moped. Amazed that the moped could pass his Ferrari, he gives it some more gas and passes the moped at 275 mph. Whoooooosh!

He's feeling pretty good until he looks in his mirror and sees the old man gaining on him again. Astounded by the speed of this old guy, he floors the gas pedal and takes the Ferrari all the way up to 320 mph. Not 10 seconds later, he sees the moped bearing down on him again. The Ferrari is going flat out and there's nothing he can do. Suddenly, the moped plows into the back of his Ferrari, demolishing the rear. The young man jumps out, and unbelievably, the old man is still alive!!! He runs up to the mangled old man and says, "Oh, my gosh! Is there anything I can do for you?"

The old man whispers with his dying breath, "Unhook my suspenders from your side-view mirror." [4]

How many of us feel like that, like we are being dragged through life? If all we need is physical rest, we can take a nap. If all we need is emotional rest, we can take a vacation. Yet where can we find spiritual rest? How can we obtain relief regarding the deepest issues of life at the deepest level of our hearts?

Even as I write about how we might enjoy the advantages of a life-giving relationship with Christ, I confess that in my own experience, finding rest can be one of the most overlooked aspects of growing my soul. Yet, finding rest in Him is significant if we want a healthy soul. Since I have engaged the role of lead pastor again, the demands on my life and my time are considerable, and there are days, even weeks, that my heartbeat is weak — my soul vaporized. I imagine God placing His spiritual stethoscope on my chest, listening for even the faintest beat of passion. Some days I just grind through the day and pray, "O God, re-kindle, renew, and restore in me an unquenchable love for you and for others. Help me see past the tasks of the day and lead me to an inspired, passionate, and fruitful ministry."

Years of ministry experience have taught me that I cannot linger in that place. I have come to understand that a nourished soul is essential for a healthy life as God places a premium on healthy living. When Jesus was asked the question, "Which is the greatest commandment in the Law?" He responded, "Love the Lord your God with all your heart and with all your soul and with all your mind" (Matthew 22:36-37, NIV). Jesus continued to emphasize that every other commandment follows after this one. In essence, until this calibrates our heart, we cannot move forward effectively.

For several months now, I have been processing through five questions. I've discovered that working periodically through these questions helps me grow my soul. I believe they will be helpful to you as well:

1. What or who is my first love?
2. To what or to whom do I listen?
3. What am I learning?
4. Am I developing my lungs?
5. Am I laughing enough?

What or who is my first love?

When God is no longer our first love, our soul becomes malnourished and we are in danger. This is why Jesus warned the church in Ephesus, "But I have this complaint against you. You don't love me or each other as you did at first! Look how far you have fallen from your first love! Turn back to me again and work as you did at first. If you don't, I will come and remove your lampstand from its place among the churches" (Revelation 2:4-5, NLT).

We are just like those first century Christians. It is easy for us to allow other things, even good things, to take first place in our lives. People who are growing their souls have a plan to identify the things that entice them into allowing something other than Christ to become their first love. We are on our way to a healthy life and a nourished soul when we make sure that God is our center. When He is our joy and

Christ reigns with no rival, we grow our soul.

What or to whom do I listen?

It's almost like a treasure hunt — I am learning how to find answers to good questions. I am very privileged to serve Des Moines First Assembly with a wonderful pastoral team. They have taught me to not just ask questions, but to ask good questions. For the most part, life consists of knowing what to do, knowing why that is important, and knowing how to bring resources to bear on the moment.

People who desire to grow their souls associate with people who have gained their experience and wisdom through their journey with Jesus. As they connect with these people, they listen, watch, and ask the right questions. Have you identified for yourself individuals who have a long journey of faithfulness and have demonstrated effectiveness in life navigation?

What am I learning?

Ed Ashby, one of our deacons, and I try to connect on a monthly basis just to encourage one another and build on our relationship outside the boardroom. Ed and his wife, Pat, founded Family Legacy Counseling here in Des Moines. They partner with people, helping them to pass down a positive legacy by developing relational and emotional health. Both Ed and Pat offer a unique viewpoint that allows them to team up with their clients, resulting in personal wholeness, more fulfilling relationships, and hope for a bright future.

One of the elements I appreciate about my time with Ed, usually over breakfast, is how we share with each other what we are learning, whether it be through sharing our life experiences or the insights gained from a new book. It is important to us that we exercise our minds. Ed has earned a Doctor of Ministry degree from Fuller Theological Seminary in California, a Master's degree in counseling from Ashland Theological Seminary in Ohio, and mental health training at Western Reserve Psychiatric Hospital. In addition, Ed served 20 years as a lead pastor. With all this in his tool belt, I believe that Ed is helpful to so many people because he is constantly learning.

It is essential to be a life-long learner if you want to grow your soul. I hope it doesn't sound like I am preaching to the choir. Well, maybe I am; you are at least reading this book. Let me affirm you in that and thank you for taking time to read this book. Actually, I want to bless you and encourage you to continue the commitment to exercise your mind. You might want to make a list of subjects about which you desire further knowledge and then identify avid readers for suggestions.

Am I developing my lungs?

You might be asking yourself, "Develop my lungs? What's that all about?" Before I continue, let me apologize for the corny alliteration of my five questions. It helps me remember them. For example, developing my lungs equates with exercise. Now, before you think I am getting too personal, be assured I am not going to suggest that you run a marathon or enter a body building contest. No, this is not an infomercial for Chuck Norris' Total Gym. However, for the next several paragraphs, I am going to suggest that a healthy body is essential to growing your soul and truly is part of enjoying the advantages of a life-giving relationship with Christ.

Because of Paul's word to Timothy, "For physical training is of some value, but godliness has value for all things . . ." (1 Timothy 4:8, NIV), many have emphasized a person's soul over the body. But Paul did not undervalue or downplay the role of physical conditioning in Timothy's life. He did not emphasize it because they walked everywhere. So if you walk everywhere and never use an escalator or elevator, please skip to the next question. The rest of you, most of you, please read on.

Today in our deskbound culture, physical exercise does matter and contributes to accomplishing God's best in our lives. The FDA advises that adults need 30 minutes of moderate exercise every day of the week. Those who are considered overweight need a minimum of 60 minutes in a regular exercise routine to start losing unwanted pounds.

Please believe me; I would not waste this page trying to connect physical conditioning with growing your soul if it was just about looking trim. God has designed us with purpose in mind. Our bodies are strategic in the activity of that purpose, and taking care of our bodies enables us to handle the stress that comes our way. When we exercise, we gain more energy to fulfill God's purpose in our lives.

I wouldn't even bring this to the table if I didn't see how it affected my life so profoundly. Eight years ago, I thought a balanced meal was one Big Mac in each hand. I was extremely overweight, suffered from fatigue, and routinely teetered on discouragement. My cholesterol was high and my physical conditioning was minimal. Today, because of my commitment to eating healthy and physical conditioning, my life is on a higher level of effectiveness and yes, even joy. My life has more dynamic, with greater energy and clarity to do what God has called me to do.

Please consider making the connection between growing your soul and physical conditioning and set some realistic exercise goals. I began this section with a statement from Paul to Timothy regarding physical discipline. Allow me to close this section with another statement by Paul:

> 19 *Or don't you know that your body is the temple of the Holy Spirit, who lives in you and was given to you by God? You do not belong to yourself,* 20 *for God bought you with a high price. So you must honor God with your body* (1 Corinthians 6:19-20, NLT).

Am I laughing enough?

"A cheerful heart is good medicine, but a broken spirit saps a person's strength" (Proverbs 17:22, NLT). I am so glad this verse is in the Bible. It suggests that God puts a premium on laughter.

Lukis, my grandson, is at the age of innocent laughter. I don't know if I have ever experienced anything so refreshing as hearing him giggle and laugh. I wonder if God is pleased when we laugh. I think so! He made sure that we understood through His Word that one of the true marks of a life-giving relationship with Him is joy (Galatians 5:22). He also made it known that His joy is our strength (Nehemiah 8:10).

Just a few days ago, I was reading an article entitled *Laughter's Link to Health May Be in the Blood*. It highlighted a study done at the University of Maryland Medical Center regarding the benefits of laughter. The study suggested that a good sense of humor and the ability to laugh at stressful situations help to mitigate the damaging physical effects of distressing emotions.

The study involved 20 healthy men and women. They were asked to watch clips of two movies — either the violent, opening battle scene in the 1998 film, *Saving Private Ryan*, or a humorous scene from a comedy, such as the 1996 *Kingpin*.

The researchers tested the subjects' vasodilatation *(widening of the lumen of blood vessels)*, before and after the movie, by constricting and releasing an artery in their arms with a blood pressure cuff and then using ultrasound to measure how the blood vessels were functioning. A striking difference was discovered, depending on which movie the volunteers had watched. Blood flow was significantly reduced in 14 of the 20 volunteers who saw the stressful film. In contrast, blood flow markedly increased in 19 of the 20 volunteers after watching the funny movie. Overall, blood flow decreased by about 35 percent after experiencing stress, but increased 22 percent after laughter — an improvement equivalent to that produced by a 15- to 30-minute workout.

Michael Miller, who led the research, said, "When you laugh you send a signal to the brain to release these endorphins, and these may activate receptors to release other chemicals, perhaps including nitric oxide, which is known to enhance blood vessel dilation." Miller and his colleagues hypothesized that laughter may also use similar mechanisms to help boost the immune system and reduce the amount of inflammation in the body, which has been linked to an increased risk of a host of health problems.[5]

According to the article, a good hearty laugh can help:
- reduce stress
- lower blood pressure
- elevate mood
- boost immune system

- improve brain functioning
- protect the heart
- connect you to others
- foster instant relaxation
- make you feel good.

Now, modern science may be validating Proverbs 17:22 — a good laugh may actually help fend off heart attacks and strokes.

Laughter is a great gift in life. It does help grow our soul. I agree with E.E. Cummings, who said, "The most wasted of all days is one without laughter."

By now, I hope you have unhooked your suspenders from the side-view mirror of the Ferrari 550, taken a deep breath, and considered Jesus' invitation to rest. As I close this chapter, I am reminded of a scene in the first book of the trilogy, *The Lord of the Rings*, where J.R.R. Tolkien portrays rest in the house of Elrond in Rivendell. The hobbits, along with Strider, their guide, have made a momentous, almost fatal journey to this place. Soon they will begin an even more perilous trek. But now, temporarily, they find rest from danger.

> *For awhile, the hobbits continued to talk and think of the past journey and of the perils*

> *that lay ahead; but such was the virtue of the land of Rivendell that soon all fear and anxiety was lifted from their minds. The future, good or ill, was not forgotten, but ceased to have power over the present. Health and hope grew strong in them, and they were content with each day as it came, taking pleasure in every meal, and in every word and song.* [6]

Did you notice the dynamics of their experience? The future, good or ill, was not forgotten, but ceased to have power over the present. This, too, is a picture of growing your soul. It takes intentionality. It requires taking time in the journey to embrace that which gives life. On this fast-paced journey called life, where and when are you stopping to take time and center your life around that which nourishes your soul?

For three years, I traveled a 10-state area as the North Regional Field Consultant for Gospel Publishing House. Because of the vast area covered on my scheduled assignments, I had a lot of windshield time. On several trips, I would drive 800 to 1,000 miles in one day. I remember one particular summer assignment when I drove from Hamilton, Montana to Chamberlin, South Dakota, a distance of about 1,000 miles. When I arrived, I took pride in that accomplishment. I actually called one of my cohorts and told him how many miles I had navigated that day. "You're going to feel it tomorrow," he said. He was right. Feel it I did! When I tried to maneuver the next morning, I hurt all over.

When my wife would accompany me, we would never make that kind of time, but I don't remember paying a heavy physical price either. Why? Because she knew how to enjoy the journey. I soon realized there is a big difference between being driven and driving.

Being driven is like the old man on the moped who is caught by something pulling him faster than he is made to go. Driving is the intentionality of stopping along the way to enjoy the journey. My wife always found some great rest stops along the way. And honestly, I remember those life-giving moments more than all the miles I logged in a single day. Where is your next stop?

Come To Me 49

3 Ask Me

16 And so they reached Jericho. Later, as Jesus and his disciples left town, a great crowd was following. A blind beggar named Bartimaeus (son of Timaeus) was sitting beside the road as Jesus was going by. 47 When Bartimaeus heard that Jesus from Nazareth was nearby, he began to shout out, "Jesus, Son of David, have mercy on me!"

48 "Be quiet!" some of the people yelled at him. But he only shouted louder, "Son of David, have mercy on me!"

49 When Jesus heard him, he stopped and said, "Tell him to come here." So they called the blind man. "Cheer up," they said. "Come on, he's calling you!"

50 Bartimaeus threw aside his coat, jumped up, and came to Jesus.

51 "What do you want me to do for you?" Jesus asked. "Teacher," the blind man said, "I want to see!"

52 And Jesus said to him, "Go your way. Your faith has healed you." And instantly the blind man could see! Then he followed Jesus down the road.

Mark 10:46-52 (NLT)

Ask Me 51

Abundance: an ample quantity, great, plenty, more than enough.

Most people do not pray; they only beg.
George Bernard Shaw

*"What do you want me to do for you?" Jesus asked.
"Teacher," the blind man said, "I want to see!"*
Mark 10:51 (NLT)

An elderly Scotsman was very ill. His minister went to see him. As he sat down by the sick man's bed, the minister noticed another chair drawn up by the other side of the bed. "Well, Donald," he said, "I see I am not your first visitor." The old man looked surprised. "I'm talking about the chair by your bed," the minister explained. "It looks like someone else has been here."

Donald said, "I want to tell you about that chair. Years ago, I found it difficult to pray. One day, I shared that with my pastor, and he told me not to worry about kneeling down. 'Just sit down,' he suggested, 'put a chair opposite you, imagine Jesus in it, and talk to Him as you would to a friend.'" The old Scotsman added, "I've been doing it ever since."

A while later, the daughter of the sick man called for the minister. When he answered, the daughter told him how her father had died very suddenly. She had no idea death was near. "I had just left him for an hour or two, for he seemed to be sleeping so comfortably. When I went back to check on him, he was dead. He had not moved since I saw him before, except that his hand was on the empty chair at the side of his bed."[1]

In light of Jesus' invitation to "Come to me," we never have to face life alone. He, the God who created the universe and all that is in it, is our companion. Think of the benefits, the advantages this companionship brings to reality. As we journey with Him, we receive the power to rise above difficulties, navigate detours, and even learn contentment in the deficiencies. These are the results of God's deep work in transforming our character.

Here are four things I have learned about prayer:

- Prayer is a dialogue with God.
- Prayer is the process by which we learn the will of God.
- Prayer is a fellowship of love with God that deepens my relationship with Him.
- Prayer changes me.

We shortchange ourselves when we view

prayer as a means of getting things for ourselves, like the parrot who relentlessly blurted out, "Let us pray." At all hours of the day and night, he would repeat the same phrase, "Let us pray." His owner did not teach him the words, nor did he understand how the parrot learned them. But over and over, the parrot would say, "Let us pray." While on a trip, the man saw a beautiful female parrot. He decided to purchase her as a companion for his other parrot. As soon as he put the new parrot in the cage, the male parrot squawked, "My prayers have been answered!"

Selfishness often creeps into our prayers. However, I take great comfort in realizing that when Jesus called His disciples to follow Him, it had little, if anything, to do with something visible in their lives and everything to do with the invisible. For a season of three years, the investment Jesus made in these men involved character transformation. He helped them acknowledge the hidden life of motives, attitudes, affections, and direction.

Have you ever wanted to see life from a new perspective? Needing to have my eyes examined for new contact lenses, I leaned back in the examination chair, closed my eyes, and waited for the doctor. I was thinking about what I had watched on television the previous day. Tiger Woods had won another golf tournament, and the commentators were talking about whether Tiger could actually perform better because of his eye surgery.

The doctor's knock and entrance were welcomed, as I was eager to ask him about this surgery. "Lasik surgery," he replied. "It is a process of reshaping the surface of the cornea to correct nearsightedness and astigmatism." All I wanted to know was whether or not it would help my golf game. I also thought it would be nice to do away with glasses and contacts.

What if there were a better way to see, that is, to see life with new vision? What if we have misinterpreted abundance? Jesus did say He came to bring life, ". . . more and better life than we ever dreamed of."[2]

Prayer is not just asking God to empower us to rise above our difficulties, help us navigate through life successfully, and make up for our deficiencies. The essential element of prayer is asking God to open our eyes that we may see beneath the surface to our hidden life, to acknowledge it, and to boldly ask Him for a transformed life. We enjoy His abundance when our hidden life corresponds with our visible life. Just before His triumphal entry, Jesus performs His last healing, as recorded by the Gospel writer,

Mark. The setting is Jericho. Mark introduces us to a blind beggar. Interestingly, Mark gives us his name, Bartimaeus.

Could it be that Mark wanted us to see that no one is too insignificant to Jesus to secure His attention? Remember, Jesus is some 18 miles from Jerusalem. While Jesus draws nearer to His impending death, He takes time to invite Bartimaeus to ask for something, "What do you want me to do for you?"

If you could have anything on earth, what would it be? What do you want most of all? What is your dream? What would make you incredibly happy? The answer to that question reveals much. "What do you want me to do for you?" may be the most important question God ever asks us. Frequently, I answer blindly, or even worse, selfishly. If I may be so vulnerable, there were times during my early days as a Christ-follower when I questioned whether my prayers did any good.

Here is what I do know:
- Jesus prayed.
- Jesus taught His disciples to pray.
- Jesus intercedes for us continually.
- My relationship with God is nourished through prayer.
- God asks me to bring my needs

to Him.
- God is omniscient, omnipresent, and omnipotent, and He is capable of doing the miraculous.
- God is always listening.
- Biblical prayer enables me to know God more intimately.

Even though he could not see where he was going, Bartimaeus made his way over to stand face to face with Jesus. "What can I do for you?" Bartimaeus could have given a number of answers to that question. He was, after all, a beggar, so he could have asked for money. Since a beggar was at the lowest end of the social ladder, he could have asked for respect and dignity. He was unable to work and could only sit and beg, so he could have asked for a job. Conversely, he did not ask for these or a myriad of other things. He simply asked, "Rabbi, I want to see."

The decibels of the animated crowd and Bartimaeus' cries for mercy must have created a rigorous moment, maybe a bit like the demanding moments of our lives. When life seems more like a blur than a blessing, it is easy to lose sight of what we really should be asking for. If we turn down the volume and reflect on the entwined happenings Mark has recorded during that eye-opening day, we may glean insight and gain the courage to ask for the right things.

Admittedly, we sometimes make poor decisions, either because we do not have adequate information or we choose to ignore the information at our disposal. Quite possibly, this is due to our failure to pay attention to both external and internal influences. The ability to ask the right question requires that we spend more time thinking beyond our limited ambitions to God's lasting abundance. What influences you?

A man approaches Jesus. He is identified by Matthew as a "young" man (Matthew 19:20) and a "ruler" by Luke (Luke 18:18). Soon, you gain the impression that he is aggressive, self-assured, and goes after what he wants. At this stage, he feels that he lacks information to achieve his goals in life, so he gathers courage to ask Jesus, "What must I do to inherit eternal life?"

I might be reading into the story line, but I believe he perceives himself as having the ability to do whatever Jesus requires. He had distinguished himself as an achiever and had climbed to the top in the past — he can do it again. Just give him the passable formula. Yet at this summit, Jesus awakens him to a spiritual reality and he mishandles the information. Why? He is spiritually blinded by his own abilities.

Prior to this encounter, Jesus had taught His disciples a surprising reality. "I tell you the truth, anyone who will not receive the kingdom of God like a little child will never enter it" (Mark 10:15, NIV). Helpless dependency on Christ rather than on our own ability is essential for entering the kingdom of God. Mark vividly recorded that the young man went away sad because he had great wealth. He was unable to navigate through the external and internal influences. Though he may have asked the right question, he did not apply the right answer.

Before that eye-opening day ebbed away, just prior to the healing of Bartimaeus, two of Jesus' disciples asked Him a question as well. "Teacher," they said, "we want you to do for us whatever we ask"(Mark 10:35, NIV). You see, earlier that day, a dispute about status and rank among the disciples was silenced by Jesus, but obviously it was not buried. These two disciples, James and John, asked Jesus to guarantee them a place at His right and left hand when He comes into His glory.

Maybe the conversation about His suffering

evaporated before it reached their hearts. All the same, they missed an important piece of information. Jesus' glory will not become completely visible to all until after the great tribulation (Mark 13:24-26). It is roughly ironic that Mark used the same language when he penned these words, "They crucified two robbers with him, one on his right and one on his left" (Mark 15:27, NIV).

That, however, was not what they were asking. They were asking for a power structure of their own. Surprisingly, Jesus responded to their selfish request with grace. "You don't know what you are asking" (Mark 10:38, NIV). He then asked them if they thought they could drink the cup that He drinks. Not understanding the implications and the intensity this cup represented, they effortlessly said, "We can" (Mark 10:39, NIV).

The other disciples became offended and annoyed at James and John's nerve — maybe more annoyed than offended because their friends' request revealed all their desires. They were irritated because James and John beat them to the punch and now held an advantage to the window of power. In the Gospel narrative, the disciples had a difficult time coming to terms with the significance of suffering and serving. They displayed a desire for power, achievement, and recognition. They did not understand that Jesus did not choose them because of their power, achievements, or ingenuity. He chose them because he saw something in them they could not see for themselves. He saw the raw potential in their hidden lives that could be redeemed.

Their misconception offered Jesus a teaching moment in which to speak into their lives about following Him. He said, in essence, that they were not relegated to "last place." Rather, He revealed to them how they could be first. They did not have to concern themselves with status when He was showing them how to be great (Mark 10:31, 42-45).

Parenthetically, the silliness of this scene forces us to examine our own requests of Christ. Does our list of requests include fancy cars, bigger homes, or comfortable lives filled with fun and fulfillment?

> *Judge a man by his questions rather than by his answers.* — François-Marie Arouet, better known by the pen name, Voltaire

In our affluent culture, we must ask ourselves the hard questions. We live in a world obsessed with position and power — a culture that says second place is first loser. When Apple's revolutionary iPhone hit the market in June of 2007, it sold for $599. Just a few weeks later, the price was reduced to $399. While some who bought the iPhone at the original prices were outraged, others would have paid any price to be the first to own the new gadget.

"If they told me at the outset the iPhone would be $200 cheaper the next day," one customer explained, "I would have thought about it for a second — and still bought it."[3]

Consumers who purchase new technology as soon as it becomes available relish the prestige of taking home a new toy before anyone else. For many, it is not the item itself but the distinction of ownership that is attractive. Such is life in "a land of plenty." Not only do we want more, we also want it first. It is no longer enough to keep up with the Joneses. We want to be the Joneses.

Many observers of the human condition have noted that we tend to live on one of three levels.[4] The first level is *survival*. For some, this survival is literal — like blind Bartimaeus, they are poor and somewhat destitute. They must spend every waking moment trying to make it through another day. Others may have full stomachs, but their survival mode is no less real. Their goal in life is simply to exist or to maintain, exacting whatever pleasures or thrills they can find in the face of a passing life.

A second level of living, slightly higher up the ladder than survival, is *success*. Some people live to make it big, like James and John in our Bible story. The problem, as you may have already discovered, is that once you arrive at this level, success really does not deliver the way you thought it would. In Arthur Miller's classic play, *Death of a Salesman*, the main character, Willy Loman, commits suicide after spending his entire life trying to be successful. His son stands by his father's grave and sadly concludes, "He had all the wrong dreams."

Fortunately, there is a third level of living that leads us beyond survival and success. This is the level of *significance*. Living a life of significance depends upon finding and following God's detailed plan. This requires open eyes. The Bible is full of people who opened their eyes to see God's purpose. I believe Bartimaeus was one of them.

As we return to the story, Mark portrays the rich young ruler and the disciples to be spiritually blind. The wide-angle lens on this day links the healing of blindness to spiritual transformation. At the beginning of Mark's story line, Jesus opens the eyes of a blind man, and the healing of Bartimaeus closes it out. Mark is helping us understand that while Jesus can heal our physical blindness, He ultimately wants to heal our spiritual blindness.

Pause for a moment and think of the rich man who would not let go of his riches and so refused to follow Christ. Remember the ambition of James and John, how they maneuvered for power and position and so missed the meaning of "the first shall be last and the last shall be first." Remember Bartimaeus. Mark skillfully communicates a clear contrast when he initially places Bartimaeus along the roadside. Jesus called for him. Follow his action:

> *Throwing his cloak aside, he jumped to his feet and came to Jesus. "What do you want me to do for you?" Jesus asked him. The blind man said, "Rabbi, I want to see." "Go," said Jesus, "Your faith has healed you." Immediately he received his sight and followed Jesus along the road* (Mark 10:50-52, NIV).

Bartimaeus voices what every Christ-follower should want — to be able to see. I believe that the moment he had new vision, he did not go back to get his cloak. The cloak he left behind was not much, but it did represent all he had. I can see him following Jesus all the way to Jerusalem shouting, "Hosanna!

Blessed is he who comes in the name of the Lord! Blessed is the coming kingdom of our father David! Hosanna in the highest!" (Mark 11:9-10, NIV).

"On February 17, 1982, the *Chicago Sun-Times* carried a story originally printed in the *Los Angeles Times* about Anna Mae Pennica, a 62-year-old woman who had been blind from birth. At age 47, she married a man she met in a braille class. For the first 15 years of their marriage, he did the seeing for both of them, until he completely lost his vision to *retinitis pigmentosa*. Mrs. Pennica had never seen the green of spring or the blue of a summer sky. Yet because she had grown up in a loving, supportive family, she never felt resentful about her handicap and always exuded a remarkably cheerful spirit.

"Then in October, 1981, Dr. Thomas Pettit of the Jules Stein Eye Institute of the University of California at Los Angeles performed surgery to remove the rare congenital cataracts from the lens of Mrs. Pennica's left eye — and she saw for the first time ever!

"The newspaper account does not record her initial response, but it does tell us that she found that everything was 'so much bigger and brighter' than she ever imagined. While she immediately recognized her husband and others she had known well, other acquaintances were taller or shorter, heavier or skinnier than she had pictured them. Since that day, Mrs. Pennica has hardly been able to wait to wake up in the morning."[5]

How stunning it must have been for Anna Mae when she saw for the first time. The physical gift of sight is wonderful. The miracle of seeing for the first time can hardly be described. Imagine how it was for Bartimaeus. At first, he was only able to hear the words of Jesus, but by the end of their conversation, he saw His face.

This whole scene recalls Isaiah's promise:

I will lead the blind by ways they have not known, along unfamiliar paths I will guide them; I will turn the darkness into light before them and make the rough places smooth. These are the things I will do; I will not forsake them (Isaiah 42:16, NIV).

What do we learn from this story? As Bartimaeus followed Jesus, he could witness the triumphal entry on Palm Sunday, the shock of the crucifixion, and the joy of the resurrection. Had he not asked for the right thing, he would have missed an eyeful.

I cannot believe I watched the entire movie,

Joe Versus the Volcano, but I am glad I did. It is a fantasy comedy pairing Meg Ryan and Tom Hanks. It was hard to resist watching Joe Banks, played by Tom Hanks, have the life sucked out of him at a dead-end job. Miserable in his gray surroundings with stark fluorescent lighting, Joe dreams of being brave again. However, a visit to the doctor reveals that he has a "brain cloud." His condition is fatal, but he will be fine for a few more months.

An eccentric millionaire, Samuel Harvey Graynamore (Lloyd Bridges), hears of Joe's predicament and comes to him with a proposal: The people of the Pacific island of Waponi Woo need a human sacrifice to appease their gods. Why not live like a king for a few weeks and then throw yourself into a volcano? (Graynamore needs a sacrificial victim to offer in exchange for permission to mine the island for a rare mineral.) Joe accepts Graynamore's lavish proposal and on his journey meets three romantic possibilities (all played by Meg Ryan).

The redeeming moment in the movie is a scene where Joe (Tom Hanks) and Patricia (Meg Ryan) are having a boat deck conversation after dinner, and she says, "My father says almost the whole world's asleep. Everybody you know, everybody you see, everybody you talk to. He says only a few people are awake. And they live in a state of constant, total amazement."[6]

Are you awake to the wonder of God? Joe, James, John, and the rich young ruler were asleep to the wonder. For Joe, it was an imaginary "brain cloud." For James and John, it was their preoccupation with self-ambition. The rich young ruler could not surrender his own importance and abilities. Regardless, they were asleep to the wonder of God.

He is truly a God of wonder in more ways than one. It amazes me that the first thing out of God's mouth, after a persistent monologue in which He speaks all of creation into existence and declares His pleasure over it, is to ask the question of the humans he created, "Where are you?" (Genesis 3:8). Does God not know the location of Adam and Eve? Of course He does, but He still asks. Why? He called them to a conversation — a relationship.

Similarly, we look at the story of Bartimaeus. Though he was sightless, his ears were attuned and his spirit awake. He heard the commotion of Jesus passing by and cried out to Him. The crowd told him to be quiet, but Jesus, hearing the cry of Bartimaeus, stopped and called for him. The crowd told Bartimaeus, "He's calling for you" (Mark 10:49). Then Jesus asked him, "What do you want me to do for you?" (Mark 10:51). There it is, an amazing new world about to be uncovered, concealed in a single question.

Jesus asks, "What do you want me to do for you?" Ponder this, until you hear Him asking you the question personally. Then, ponder it further until you can give an answer.

Christ invites us to enjoy a transformed life – living abundantly within His providential care. But spiritual transformation is not about closing the deal like the hopeful, rich young ruler or attaining certain levels of status like James and John. On the contrary, it is all about making the journey. When we pray for the right things with the right motives, God will give us abundant life — amazing, abundant life. Open your eyes and live in total amazement.

The Bible invites us to trust Christ and then to speak up rather than close up. Here are just a few of His invitations:

- *Base your happiness on your hope in Christ. When trials come, endure them patiently, steadfastly maintain the habit of prayer* (Romans 12:12, Phillips NT).
- *Devote yourselves to prayer with an alert mind and a thankful heart* (Colossians 4:2, NLT).

- *One day Jesus told His disciples a story to illustrate their need for constant prayer and to show them that they must never give up* (Luke 18:1, NLT).
- *Pray at all times and on every occasion in the power of the Holy Spirit. Stay alert and be persistent in your prayers for all Christians everywhere* (Ephesians 6:18, NLT).
- *Everything will soon come to an end. So be serious and be sensible enough to pray* (1 Peter 4:7, CEV).
- *But you, dear friends, build yourselves up in your most holy faith and pray in the Holy Spirit* (Jude 20, NIV).

4 Remain In Me

5 Yes, I am the vine; you are the branches. Those who remain in me, and I in them, will produce much fruit. For apart from me you can do nothing. 6 Anyone who parts from me is thrown away like a useless branch and withers. Such branches are gathered into a pile to be burned. 7 But if you stay joined to me and my words remain in you, you may ask any request you like, and it will be granted! 8 My true disciples produce much fruit. This brings great glory to my Father.

9 I have loved you even as the Father has loved me. Remain in my love. 10 When you obey me, you remain in my love, just as I obey my Father and remain in his love. 11 I have told you this so that you will be filled with my joy. Yes, your joy will overflow! 12 I command you to love each other in the same way that I love you. 13 And here is how to measure it — the greatest love is shown when people lay down their lives for their friends. 14 You are my friends if you obey me. 15 I no longer call you servants, because a master doesn't confide in his servants. Now you are my friends, since I have told you everything the Father told me. 16 You didn't choose me. I chose you. I appointed you to go and produce fruit that will last, so that the Father will give you whatever you ask for, using my name. 17 I command you to love each other.

John 15:5-17 (NLT)

Friend: one attached to another by affection or esteem, one that is not hostile, one that is of the same nation, party, or group, one that favors or promotes something, a favored companion.

Tell me what company thou keepst, and I'll tell thee what thou art.
Miguel de Cervantes (1547 - 1616)
Spanish novelist

During our first few years of marriage, my wife and I faithfully watched Magnum P.I. For many, Tom Selleck, playing the role of Thomas Magnum, a private investigator, was the main draw. Yet Higgins was a unique character who drew my interest. He was a bit mysterious, bordering on bogus, with all those war stories about Burma. Most likely, he never was in Burma, but I liked him.

I never bought the story line. There was a huge estate in Hawaii belonging to Robin Masters, who was supposed to arrive soon for a visit. He never came. Higgins was always worried sick that Robin Masters would come home and fire him for something he had done wrong.

Higgins allowed Magnum to stay at the estate without paying rent. He let Magnum use the Ferrari, which was wrecked about every other episode. They held huge garden parties and had dogs running all over the garden, digging up plants. In about every third or fourth episode, somebody would come with an Uzi and machine gun the estate. Yet Higgins was never fired.

In the last episode, Magnum, standing next to Higgins, said, "Oh, by the way, Higgins, I've been meaning to ask you a question. Are you Robin Masters?" Of course, Higgins was Robin Masters (although this theory was never fully proven), but that was the last line of the show.

Although Magnum's carefree ways often clashed with Higgins' stricter manner, their mutual respect formed a strong basis for the development of a friendship.

Who can live without friendship? Jesus called a rag-tag group of men to follow him; eventually these men would transition from followers to friends. In the Scriptures, Jesus did not refer to these men as His "friends" until John 15 (NLT). Jesus talks in a straightforward way about the relationship between His power and their connectedness to Him. "Remain in me, and I will remain in you" (v. 4a). Jesus went on to warn them they could not be productive unless they were connected to Him. "For a branch cannot produce fruit if it is severed from the vine, and you cannot be fruitful apart from me" (v. 4b).

Jesus often used things at hand to illustrate or explain spiritual truths. For example, in John 7, as the priest approached the altar and was pouring out the symbolic water, Jesus exclaimed, "If anyone is thirsty, let him come to me and drink." The next day, in John 8, as Jesus stood in the temple treasury before massive, snuffed-out torches that symbolized the pillar of fire in the wilderness, He said, "I am the light of the world. Whoever follows me will never walk in darkness, but will have the light of life." He used those snuffed-out torches to proclaim that He was the glory of God.

In the same symbolic manner, Jesus used a grapevine as an illustration of spiritual truth in John 15. The fact that Israel was often referred to as a vine reinforced His use of this image. In essence, the energy of His expression was, "You all know how Israel is pictured as a vine that is meant to produce refreshing fruit. Well, I am the realization of all that symbol suggests."

One can imagine that they must have hung on every word He spoke. It is in the midst of this conversation that Jesus states that remaining in Him will result in a maximizing impact.

For you and me, this is a delightfully deep

and mystic metaphor. Christ is the vine, we are the branches, and God the Father is the gardener. The portrait is that of a vineyard with fully-devoted friends of Jesus organically related to Him and of God the Father walking among the vines, lovingly caring for them so they will bring forth fruit. The prevailing emphasis of Jesus is true; pure friendship with Him is fruit-bearing, as we see in verses 2, 3, 4, 5 and 8:

> *2 He cuts off every branch that doesn't produce fruit, and he prunes the branches that do bear fruit so they will produce even more. 3 You have already been pruned for greater fruitfulness by the message I have given you. 4 Remain in me, and I will remain in you. For a branch cannot produce fruit if it is severed from the vine, and you cannot be fruitful apart from me.*
>
> *5 Yes, I am the vine; you are the branches. Those who remain in me, and I in them, will produce much fruit. For apart from me you can do nothing.*
>
> *8 My true disciples produce much fruit. This brings great glory to my Father.*

Jesus wanted His friends to know that they could go in their own strength, their own power, and their own abilities, but they would miss out on God's strength, God's power, and God's abilities. And that would be too much to miss!

Yet, that is exactly what Peter did — he missed it. Just hours following this moment packed with intimate symbolism, Peter reacted in his own strength and skill. He furiously pulled out his sword and struck the high priest guard, cutting off his ear. It is interesting that almost immediately afterwards, Peter denied Christ three times.

It reminds me of the young man who had worked for years on the railroad and wanted to move up to the position of signalman. For his interview, he was told to meet the inspector at the signal box. The inspector asked him, "What would you do if you realized that two trains were heading toward each other on the same track?" The young man replied, "That's easy. I would change the track that one of the trains was traveling on." The inspector asked, "What if the lever was broken?" The young man said, "Then I would jump down out of the signal box and I would use the manual lever over there." Next the inspector asked, "What if the lever had been struck by lightening?" The young man replied, "Then I would run down to the public emergency phone and call the next signal box and tell them what was happening." The inspector continued, "What if the public phone had been vandalized and could not be used?" The young man replied, "Then I would run into town and get my uncle." That answer puzzled the inspector, so he asked, "Why would you go get your uncle?" The young man replied, "That's simple. Because he has never seen a train wreck."

Jesus said that apart from Him we can do nothing. Try as we may, when we navigate through life thinking we are pulling all the right levers, making all the right moves, and making wise choices, eventually, without Christ, we will crash.

We all need to do a careful examination of our lives as to fruit-bearing. Most of us immediately think about what we have been doing for the Lord — a subtle temptation is to substitute our activity for God in place of our friendship with God. I have heard this pattern likened to cut flowers. We try to maintain our life and fruitfulness, but we are cut off from our root. We want power to meet the demands of life without prayer, dynamic results without devotion, and abundance from God without abiding in Christ. Just like the cut flowers, we try to maintain our appearance — we add water, yet it is only a matter of time before we wither and die.

Through the prophet Jeremiah, God asked an extremely important question: "Who is he who will devote himself to be close to me?" (Jeremiah 30:21, NIV). Only when we live in close relation and communion with Christ can the God-given purposes of our lives be truly energized. We need to be in vital friendship with Christ in order to maximize our impact in this world.

Jesus was not equating activity with bearing fruit; rather, fruit is evidenced by the reproduction of the life of the vine in the branch. Jesus is looking for the fruit of His life in us. If the inward graces of the Holy Spirit, ". . . love, joy, peace, patience, kindness, goodness, faithfulness, gentleness and self-control" (Galatians 5:22-23), are not present (not perfected, but present) in our lives, we must face the fact that we may not have transitioned from distant follower to true friend.

In the next few pages, I want to inventory how our friendship with Christ impacts our lives. What happens to a person who remains in Christ? As we are connected to Him, what will He do to, through, and for us? Allow me to highlight the outcomes of our friendship with Christ.

First, it makes us more like Him, as there must be something of the life of the vine in us if we belong to God! There must be Christ-likeness.

In addition, the inward graces of the Spirit will, in time, bring the outward fruit — maximizing our influence with the culture.

Thirdly, our friendship with Christ brings to bear a new relational dynamic with others.

The first outcome of our friendship with Christ is that we grow to be like Him.

James Michener shares in his novel, *The Source*, a fascinating story of a Canaanite tribesman name Urbaal. In this story, Urbaal and his wife, Timna, are visited by the priests of their pagan Canaanite faith. They are asked to submit their firstborn son to be sacrificed in worship of their god, Makor. It would have been blasphemous for Urbaal and Timna to refuse to surrender their infant son to the arms of this child-consuming god of the Canaanites. With great anguish, they gave up their son.

As Timna watched in horror her son being consumed by the fire, the tribesmen stood around the altar of the high priest, as one would be chosen to spend a week with the new prostitute priestess. Their fertility gods demanded that one man be chosen from the village to live with this cult prostitute priestess for a week. Because his first son had been offered as a sacrifice to Makor, Urbaal was a candidate in the election. When his name was drawn, Timna was emotionally crushed by the obvious delight on Urbaal's face.

As she turned and walked away from the scene and her husband departed to live with the priestess, Timna could not hold back her anguish over the sight of their only baby boy being consumed in the fire of the pagan idol. Timna made a profound statement: "He would have been a very different man if he had a different god."[1]

What are you becoming, based upon your view of God? What images come to mind when you hear the name "Jesus"?

My journey toward a healthy relationship with God had been a rough one. I grew up somewhat afraid of God. I thought He was always angry with me. The preaching I grew up with was harsh and demanding. It seemed like all the preachers were angry at something. The concept that God was the Son of Man who embraced me with His love and disarmed me with His grace was far from my understanding.

My image of God was not of someone who wanted to be my friend. It was the greatest day of my life when I discovered that one of the chief purposes of my life was to be His friend!

How you view Jesus greatly impacts you. As I invest time now enjoying my friendship with Christ, I find myself confronted with His words and actions through the Scriptures. These encounters create a longing to know Him better.

During his days as president, Thomas Jefferson and a group of companions were traveling across the country on horseback. They came to a river which had left its banks because of a recent downpour. The swollen river had washed out the bridge, leaving each rider to ford the river on horseback, fighting for his life against the rapid currents. The very real possibility of death threatened each rider, which caused a traveler who was not part of their group to step aside and watch. After several had plunged in and made it to the other side, the stranger asked President Jefferson if he would ferry him across the river. The president agreed without hesitation. The man climbed on, and shortly thereafter the two of them made it safely to the other side. As the stranger slid off the back of the saddle onto dry ground, one in the group asked him, "Tell me, why did you select the President to ask this favor of?" The man was shocked, admitting he had no idea it was the President who had helped him. "All I know," he said, "is that on some of your faces was written the answer 'No,' and on some of them was the answer 'Yes.' His was a 'Yes' face."[2]

Jesus is a friend with a "yes" face! His "yes" enables us to become like Him. Transformation is a buzzword today, which is a good thing. We need transformation, but we cannot change by ourselves. We need help. Jesus promised to transform us, but we must stay connected to Him. Becoming like Him is a reality of friendship with Him. We have a divine and mysterious partnership with Christ.

A character in C. S. Lewis's *Chronicles of Narnia* series, Eustace Scrub, provides a poignant picture of the transformation a partnership with Christ produces in one's life. Eustace is a selfish, immature boy who thinks only of himself. In *The Voyage of the Dawn Treader*, he not only finds himself in a dragon's cave, but he also discovers he has turned into a dragon! He attempts to remove the scales but cannot do so by himself. Finally the Lion, the Christ-figure, comes. Eustace describes what happens next:

> *This is what the Lion said, but I don't know if he spoke. "You will have to let me undress*

you." I was afraid of his claws I can tell you, but I was pretty nearly desperate, so I just lay flat on my back and let him do it. The very first tear he made was so deep that I thought it had gone right to my heart and when he began pulling the skin off it hurt worse than anything I had ever felt. The only thing that made me able to bear it was just the pleasure of feeling the stuff peel off.[3]

That is how it is when we partner with Christ. We would rather do it ourselves, but we cannot. Even if we could, we would not remove what really has to go. The truth is, what is noble and attractive in us has come from the cutting we would have avoided.

In chapter one, we discovered the promise of rest Christ gives to those who come to Him. In the same way, we see that He will faithfully fulfill His role in our partnership with Him in that He prunes the branches that do bear fruit so they will produce even more (John 15:2, NLT).

While I was trying to write this chapter, I was attending a pastors' forum on world missions in San Diego, California. My schedule opened up, affording me the opportunity to extend my stay for a few extra days. What do you do in the winter when you live in the Midwest, you like to golf, you are distracted from writing, and you have a few days in sunny San Diego? Call for a tee time!

On my way to the golf course, I passed by several vineyards. As I made my way around the winding hillside, I noticed miles of bare, twisted trunks. I thought for a moment – if it were summer, instead of twisted trunks I would see endless rows of lush green grapevines. Why? Because, in the winter the vines are pruned so the main stock will have more advantageous growth and fruit in the spring. My thought processes were interrupted when I turned the corner and saw the entrance sign to the golf course. I could hardly wait to get to the tee box and pull out my driver for the first time in four months. As I walked the fairways that day, my thoughts of the vineyards returned, and I whispered a prayer of gratefulness. I was grateful for the faithfulness of Jesus in my life to prune back my branches.

Days later, when I returned to my office and watched the snow pile up outside my window, I wondered how long it would be before I could hit a golf ball down a green fairway once again. For some strange reason, as I was thinking about spring and summer, this thought came to me, "Will I be more like Jesus a few months from now, because today I am allowing His pruning knife to cut away that which He chooses?" It was almost as if God wanted me to linger on the vineyard illustration. I could not let it go, so I began to do some research on pruning.

Grape-growers, viticulturists as they call themselves, practice several stages of pruning. One particular stage intrigued me. Pinching, as it is called, involves the gardener removing the growing tip or new growth of the plant so it will not grow too rapidly. This is the least damaging method of pruning and is the gardener's first opportunity to control the plant. It encourages proper growth in the plant by removing its terminal growth or lateral growth.[4]

Some of us have been conditioned to believe that if we hustle enough, if we produce enough, or if we sell enough, then our bosses or our parents or our spouses will love us. We make the same mistake as Christians in thinking that if we read the Bible two hours a day and fast three days a week, if we are good and pure and righteous and spiritual and honest and sweet and loving and kind, if we go to church every time the doors are open, or if we have a big, black Bible that we carry everywhere we go, God will love us. One of the most dangerous lies believed by Christians is that production produces acceptance.

I want to suggest that this attitude needs to be pinched. This attitude produces activity that is basically terminal or lateral growth, not true transformational growth. When we try to produce fruit from our own activity, we surrender to a subtle seduction that says our action produces fruit. Believe me, it just produces more activity. Production does not produce acceptance. Acceptance produces acceptance. Jesus works on the inside, pinching back premature growth produced by our own ingenuity. Transformational growth (becoming Christ-like) is the result of simply accepting Christ's work in us and allowing His inward graces to permeate our inner life.

Darryl Stingley's life illustrates the working of Christ's inward graces. Stingley was declared dead in a Chicago hospital on April 5, 2007, after being found unresponsive in his home. He was 55. He spent 29 years of his life in a wheelchair, and his death was related to an injury he suffered on August 12, 1978, when as a top receiver for the New England Patriots, he was leaping for a pass thrown by quarterback Steve Grogan. Jack Tatum of the Oakland Raiders laid a hit on him that broke Darryl's neck and left him a quadriplegic.

When the press interviewed Stingley 10 years

after his injury, he said, "I have relived that moment over and over again. I was 26 years old at the time, and I remember thinking, "What's going to happen to me? If I live, what am I going to be like? And then there were all those Whys, whys, whys?" He then commented, "It was only after I stopped asking why, that I was able to regroup and go on with my life."

A crucial part of moving on was forgiving Jack Tatum, the Oakland Raider who had ended Stingley's career. Tatum hit violently, and his style of play has been debated in football circles for years. He even wrote a book entitled *Final Confessions of an NFL Assassin*. Though disturbed by reading that it was Tatum's intent to hurt those on the opposing team, Darryl Stingley forgave the man who changed his life. "For me to go on and adapt to a new way of life," Stingley said, "I had to forgive him. I couldn't be productive if my mind was clouded by revenge or animosity."

When Darryl learned Jack Tatum had to have part of a leg amputated because of diabetes, he felt for him. When interviewed by *The Boston Globe* in 2003, Stingley said, "You can't, as a human being, feel happy about something like that happening to another human being. Maybe the natural reaction is to think he got what was coming to him, but I don't accept human nature as our real nature. Human nature teaches us to hate. God teaches us to love."[5]

As stated earlier, when Jesus talked about fruit, he emphasized the process of becoming more like Him. God promises to transform us from our own image into the image of Christ.

The second outcome of our friendship with Christ is having a greater influence in our culture.

We have processed what friendship with Jesus does to us, but what will He do through us? Jesus said to His disciples, "I appointed you to go and produce fruit that will last, so that the Father will give you whatever you ask for, using my name" (John 15:16). Early that day, Jesus had encouraged them with certainty that they would do what He had done, and even greater things would be accomplished if they exercised faith in Him (John 14:12). Greater than You, Jesus? Yes!

Jesus is a friend who delights in our success. The emphasis of Jesus' barely credible, predictive words indicated He would give the disciples greater power for the miraculous, greater love to extend, greater hope to share, greater service to offer, and greater opportunities for influence.

Do you remember reading of the time Jesus

sent out 72 of His followers? They were to go two-by-two on a tour through the villages surrounding Capernaum in Galilee. Incredible things took place. They returned to Jesus full of amazement and said, "Lord, even the demons obey us when we use your name!" (Luke 10:17, NLT). Jesus celebrated their success, knowing that this was only the first of many remarkable opportunities and challenges awaiting His friends.

What do you think about this idea of being commissioned to greater things? The fact that Jesus champions our influence in our culture should cause us to rely on Him for creativity and believe that greater things can only be accomplished in His name. Our part is to pray and believe and to attempt great things for God as we go into our culture. "I appointed you to go . . ." (John 15:16, NLT).

This suggests that we must be prepared to live adventurously with diversity and paradox. As we venture into our culture, we will soon discover, if we haven't already, that it is a confused and messy place. Nevertheless, God has not abandoned it — He is present behind the scenes. He is there before we arrive!

This fragmented culture presents daunting challenges, yet it also provides a fertile environment in which the seed of the Gospel can take root. Big change came into our lives because of Jesus Christ. Out of that experience, we want to persuade others. This will entail our coming to a fresh understanding that the church experience is not just for the Christ-follower but also for the world that Jesus came to save.

Let me suggest two ideas to influence our culture: *Invite* and *Invest*.

A recent survey done in England offers insight into the minds of those who do not attend church and ideas for reaching the seemingly unreachable. Most of those surveyed agreed that the strongest motivating factor for attending a worship service would be the personal invitation of a family member or friend. Other prime motivators: a more general church invitation (like a phone call or a flyer), difficult personal circumstances, personal illness, or a time of depression. The survey found that openness to alternative worship structures and special mid-week gatherings also catch the eye of the seeker. England's "Fresh Expressions" movement is proving quite effective in its experimentation with church traditions, attracting young and old alike, modern or postmodern.

Some churches in England have created a

special "Back to Church" Sunday, inviting "lapsed" attendees to come back and reconsider commitment. More than 20 churches in the London area have adopted this as a regular event during their calendar year. Though outreach efforts have sometimes seen mixed results — and though some surveyed say they will never attend any worship service whatsoever — a few of these ideas seem to be working. Worship around Christmas has increased by a third since 2000. Easter celebrations have seen a 9 percent rise in the same period of time. Overall, worship attendance in London cathedrals has increased by 17 percent.[6]

Thom S. Rainer and Sam S. Rainer III, in *Getting to Know Today's Unchurched*, indicate a distinct receptivity among the unchurched population. In fact, about 38 percent of the unchurched are receptive or highly receptive to attending church. The reason they do not attend is that they have yet to be invited. If invited and escorted, 82 percent of the unchurched we surveyed are open to attending church with a friend or acquaintance. Unfortunately, only 21 percent of active church-going Christians invited someone to church last year.

This affords you and me a great opportunity, as one of the most saddening discoveries of this research revealed that most of the unchurched adults commented that no one had ever presented the Gospel to them! Very few of those outside the church have ever had anyone, much less a neighbor, share their faith with them.[7]

While many of us may fall into the trap of believing that those who do not attend a church have a negative perception of church, the opposite is true. Most of the unchurched have a positive view of pastors, other ministers, and church as a whole. Such positive perceptions should be an encouragement for the local church to be outwardly focused.

The exciting part of this research is the simplicity of reaching the myriad of people not attending a local church. More importantly, the opportunity is there for sharing the Gospel when we are obedient to the calling of the Great Commission.

We all have a desire to be treated with courtesy and hospitality. Having people over for a meal and truly making the effort to get to know them can build a relationship and make it easier to invite them to church.

Whether from fear of rejection or not knowing what to say, we often struggle to publicize the transforming message of the Gospel. The early Christians, on the other hand, could not keep quiet about Jesus! Because the first believers were generous, uniquely different, and courageous, they earned the respect of outsiders and influenced them to a new way of life.

In the same way, our outreach (inviting and investing) will be most effective if we first get beyond ourselves and then believe God will meet us in the culture. As long as we are faithful to the message of the Gospel, God will champion our success. The previously highlighted story of the early disciples reminds us that when the Lord transforms your life, appoints you to go, and promises your success, it is impossible to keep silent.

In 1999, my son Levi was attending college in Washington, and during a phone conversation, he asked me if I had heard of John Grisham and his series of books. I told him I had heard of him but had not read any of his books. Well, Levi's enthusiasm prompted me to get a copy of *The Testament*. Upon reading it straight through, I understood Levi's appetite for Grisham's work.

John Grisham had written earlier books, such as *A Time To Kill*, dating back to 1989. It sold just 5,000 copies in hard cover. I don't think it was advertised, nor did it ever make a list or receive any reviews that I am aware of. It was sort of a flop.

Then, he wrote *The Firm*, which was not advertised either. It was hardly reviewed, and the reviews it did receive were not very good. But people read it, liked it, and told other people they liked it. As a result, *The Firm* sold seven million copies. (It didn't hurt that they sold the movie rights to Paramount.)

John Grisham has written many other books, and today he enjoys the perks of several best sellers. All of this happened, not because of advertising or a publisher's clever marketing plan, but because many people liked his books and told other people about his writing.

We are people who like Jesus. We have experienced Him, so we tell somebody else. It does not take a newspaper ad or a review in a magazine. Evangelism is people who like Jesus and have experienced Him telling other people, until it has spread to thousands and millions and tens of millions and hundreds of millions and more.

Our greatest opportunity for the *greater things* is our stories of transformation. When evangelism becomes an invitation to friendship, the world will take notice of our investment in them. Yes, the message of the Cross is offensive to this fragmented, fearful, and factitious world, so we should not be surprised by some conflict. However, when our message is Jesus, God is our champion, and we have the power to do the greater things.

The third outcome of our friendship with Christ is a new relational dynamic with other believers.

Billy and Willie, twin sons of a merchant in the Midwest, were inseparable companions. From the beginning, they dressed alike, went to the same schools, and did everything together. They even went to work in their father's store, and when he died, they co-owned and operated the business. Uniquely, neither of them married, and their relationship to each other was pointed to as a model of creative collaboration.

One morning, a customer came into the store and made a small purchase, a dollar's worth of merchandise. Billy waited on him, placing the dollar bill on top of the cash register so he could walk to the front door with the man. Some time later, he remembered what he had done, but when he went to the cash register, the dollar was gone. Billy mused, "That's strange. I distinctly remember putting it on the cash register." He asked Willie if he had put the dollar in the cash register, but Willie declared he had not seen the dollar.

Perhaps if the matter had been dropped at

that point — a mystery involving a tiny amount of money — nothing would have come of it. Unfortunately, Billy brought it up again an hour later, this time with a barb of accusation. "Willie, are you sure you didn't do something with that dollar bill?" Willie was quick to catch the note of accusation and flared back in defensive anger. A fight ensued, and for the first time, a serious breach of trust came between these two. It grew wider and wider. Every time they tried to discuss the issue, new charges and countercharges got mixed into the brew, until finally things got so bad that they were forced to dissolve their partnership. In fact, they ran a partition down the middle of their father's store and turned what had once been a harmonious partnership into a vicious competition. Each one tried to turn the people in the community against the other, and their former model relationship became a source of division in the whole community. This polarization and bitterness went on for more than 20 years.

Then one day, a car with an out-of-state license plate parked in front of the store. A well-dressed man got out, went into one of the doors to the store, and asked Billy how long the merchant had been in business in that location. When the man learned it was more than 20 years, the stranger said, "Then you are the one with whom I must settle an old debt."

"Some 20 years ago," he said, "I was out of work, drifting from place to place, and I happened to get off a box car in your town. I had absolutely no money and had not eaten for three days. As I was walking down the alley behind your store, I looked in and saw a dollar bill on top of the cash register. Everyone else was in the front of the store. I had been raised in a Christian home, and I had never before in all my life stolen anything, but that morning I was so hungry that I gave in to the temptation, slipped through the door, and took that dollar bill. That act has weighed on my conscience ever since, and I finally decided that I would never be at peace until I came back and faced up to that old sin and made amends. Would you let me now replace that money and pay you whatever is appropriate for damages?"

The stranger tried to hand Billy a large sum of money, but he couldn't, for Billy was shaking his head in dismay and dissolving into tears. When Billy gained control of himself, he took the stranger by the arm and said, "I want you to go next door, and repeat the same story you have just told me." When the stranger told Willie the story, both began to weep uncontrollably, not so much because of what the stranger had done to them, but because of what they had done to each other in response to his action.[8]

If you are like me, you never thought that sustaining relationships would be so difficult. As a kid, it never occurred to me to "work" on any of my relationships. They just happened. Sure, there was the occasional "picking up my marbles" and going home or being the one left startled when another boy picked up his marbles. But the next day, everything was good.

Somewhere along the line, I entered the scrimmage of mature relationships, and things became unpredictable. I discovered some people were more difficult, if not impossible, to get along with. I quickly learned, for example, that trusted friends could betray me. Authority figures that I admired could ignore me. A peer's constant criticism could wound me. I also learned that unless I wanted to live a lonely existence, I could not walk away from every relationship that hit a snag.

Eleanor Doan, educator and author, was quoted in *Speakers Sourcebook* as saying, "Irritation in the heart of a believer is always an invitation to the devil to stand by."

We are tremendously fortunate that Jesus did not isolate the vineyard metaphor on our connectedness with Him. John 15:12-17 focuses on the friendship and love that are to exist among the branches of the vine. Actually, all of chapter 15 is concerned with the believer's relationships.

We have already highlighted that the relationship between the vine and the branches is representative of Christ and His followers, His *friends*. Additionally, the outcome of that connection between the vine and the branches is of great impact to the culture and to the world. Now, verses 12-17 accent the relationship of branch to branch, or believer to believer. With great imagery, Jesus heightens the importance of experiencing loving relationships with one another.

A true friend of Jesus (a branch connected to the vine) will prioritize essential qualities of relational vitality that lead to genuine love for others. As I write, I find myself dreaming about the "what if" of the Christian experience. For example, what if we were truly known for our love? What if the world saw only our mutuality of heart when they looked at us? What if all the lost people in listening range of our conversations only heard love and affirmation from our lips? What if our tough love was also a tender love? What if our love for each other was filled with gratitude, grace, and generosity? That expression of love is what Jesus commanded and is the brand of love He longed for His disciples to exemplify. "I command you to love each other in the same way that I love you" (John 15:12). Yet the contrast between that love and what is evidenced so often around us is startling.

Some time ago, I read somewhere that our experiences with one another in the church are likened to the fairy tale of a frog that was not a frog but, in reality, a prince. We all know how the fairy tale goes. A wicked witch had cast a spell on the prince, and only the kiss of a beautiful maiden could save him. There he sat for the longest time — an unkissed prince in frog form.

Charles Swindoll has written, "Do you ever feel like a frog? Frogs feel slow and low, ugly and putty, drooped, and pooped. I know. One told me. The frog feeling comes when you want to be bright but you are dumb. When you want to share, but you are selfish. When you want to be thankful, but you are filled with resentment. When you want to be great, but you are small. When you want to care, but you are indifferent. Yes, at one time or another each of us has found himself on a lily pad, floating down the great river of life, frightened and disgusted but too frightened to budge."[9]

I believe we all want to experience the benefits

of Jesus' brand of love, yet for many, self-absorption stands in the way of committing to loving and caring relationships. We are in frog form. We are in need of love's kiss.

What is love's task? Staying with the analogy, kissing frogs, of course, and allowing ourselves to be kissed. The principle of loving others as Christ loves us is beautiful.

As we remain in Christ, realizing that apart from Him we can do nothing, we will love the branches. Many believers will not reach their potential without affirmation, grace, and partnership. Here's a *what if*: Think of how we would reach unimaginable heights if only someone would say, "I know you are really a prince!"

In 1982, *Sports Illustrated* highlighted a great story about a young boy who participated in a Special Olympics race in South Bend, Indiana. His name was Wally Robinshaw. Five boys were at the starting line, ready to race. Moments before the race began, however, Wally decided to look straight up . . . into the sky. The two line judges could not believe what they saw. The race was about to start, and the other four boys had followed Wally's gaze by looking into the sky. And then, like a wave through the entire stadium, everybody in the crowd starting gazing upward.

Wally decided he was finished looking at the sky, and at that very moment, the gun went off. Wally took off running, but just a few feet from the finish line, he turned around, only to see that he was the only one running. The other four boys were still gazing into the sky.

Wally stopped and yelled, "Hey guys, c'mon, there's nothing up there; c'mon let's go!" The other boys took off, and Wally got more excited, as he cheered them on. He got totally caught up in the excitement of the race. "C'mon, you can do it," he shouted.

As he was clapping and cheering, the four boys ran right past him and crossed the finish line. Wally came in dead last. *Sports Illustrated* wrote, "Wally Robinshaw wanted to win, but even more, Wally wanted to race."

That night at the Special Olympics banquet, an award was given to the boy who most represented the "Spirit of the Games" . . . and the winner was Wally Robinshaw. The presenter said, "Show me a person with the heart and spirit of Wally. Show me a person who's not afraid to allow others to pass him by, and cheer them on . . . and I will show you a winner."[10]

We can group ourselves into two categories, marbles or grapes. Marbles are single units that do not affect each other except in collision. Grapes, on the other hand, mingle juices; each one is a part of the fragrance of the church body.

The early followers of Christ did not bounce around like loose marbles going in all different directions. Picture them as a cluster of grapes squeezed together by their mutuality of heart for Christ. If we roll in and out of our church experience each week without any grape juice stains, we really are not connected to the vine.

Ralph Emerson wrote, "Happiness is a perfume you cannot pour on others without getting a few drops on yourself."

In John 15:9-12, Jesus says:

9 *I have loved you even as the Father has loved me. Remain in my love.* 10 *When you obey me, you remain in my love, just as I obey my Father and remain in his love.* 11 *I have told you this so that you will be filled with my joy. Yes, your joy will overflow!* 12 *I command you to love each other in the same way that I love you.*

When our relationship with God is what it ought to be, it is remarkable. We become like Him, have greater influence in our culture, and experience a new relational dynamic with other believers.

5 Depend On Me

13 *When Jesus came to the region of Caesarea Philippi, he asked his disciples, "Who do people say that the Son of Man is?"* 14 *"Well," they replied, "some say John the Baptist, some say Elijah, and others say Jeremiah or one of the other prophets."* 15 *Then he asked them, "Who do you say I am?"* 16 *Simon Peter answered, "You are the Messiah, the Son of the living God."*

17 *Jesus replied, "You are blessed, Simon son of John, because my Father in heaven has revealed this to you. You did not learn this from any human being.* 18 *Now I say to you that you are Peter, and upon this rock I will build my church, and all the powers of hell will not conquer it.* 19 *And I will give you the keys of the Kingdom of Heaven. Whatever you lock on earth will be locked in heaven, and whatever you open on earth will be opened in heaven."*

Matthew 16:13-19 (NLT)

Mission: a specific task with which a person or a group is charged.

Here is the test to find whether your mission on earth is finished. If you're alive, it isn't.
Richard Bach

Believe and act as if it were impossible to fail.
Charles F. Kettering

Yogi Berra, the well-known catcher for the New York Yankees, and Hank Aaron, who, prior to Barry Bonds, was the all-time leading home run hitter and at the time played for the Milwaukee Braves, were playing each other in the World Series. The year was 1958 and, as usual, Yogi was keeping up the chatter intended to encourage his teammates while distracting the Milwaukee batters.

As Aaron came to the plate, Yogi said, "Henry, you're holding the bat wrong! You're supposed to hold it so you can read the trademark."

Aaron looked at him but didn't say a word. On the very next pitch, he hit a double. Later that inning, upon crossing home plate, Hank Aaron looked at Yogi Berra and said, "I didn't come up here to read."[1]

To succeed in a mission, you must know

why you are standing at the plate. The number of ways that churches and church leaders manage to become distracted from mission-critical priorities constantly amazes and concerns me, especially when Jesus so clearly defined and outlined the mission of the church.

Loren Mead wrote, "Where a sense of mission has been clear and compelling, the church has been sacrificial and heroic in its support of that mission."[2]

Matthew describes for us the situation surrounding the disciples when they received the first phase of their mission to build the New Testament church. Think with me as we review that point in time.

They were somewhere on a dirt road near the city of Caesarea Philippi when Jesus asked His disciples two questions. First, "Who do people say I am?" They responded with the names they had heard from the average people on the street. The rural community of Nazareth had said he was only the son of Joseph, the carpenter, yet they acknowledged they could not account for His wisdom and His mighty actions. Throughout the region of Galilee, it was admitted that He was something more, but who He was had generated some animated discussion. The average Joe along the dirt road thought Jesus was great. They were impressed with His teaching, but they did not comprehend that He was the Son of God.

Now Jesus had the disciples' interest; He had set them up for the second question, "Who do you say I am?" Perhaps they were silent for a moment and tried not to look uncertain. Then Peter broke the silence. Unlike the other times when he spoke up and embarrassed himself, this time he offered a Spirit-led confession and momentous affirmation, "You are the Christ, the Son of the living God" (Matthew 16:16, NIV).

Peter's recognition and confession of Jesus as the Christ is fundamental for us in responding to God's mission for the church. When Jesus claims, "On this rock," it is on the confession of people, like Peter, who see Jesus as the promised deliverer of God, that the church will be built (Matthew 16:18).

In his commentary on Matthew and Mark, J. W. McGarvey brings to our attention the force of the future tense of Jesus' declaration, "I will build." He observes that it was not, "I have built," nor, "I am building," but, "I will build." The cornerstone itself, Jesus Christ, had yet to be fitted and laid in its place by His death, burial, and resurrection.[3]

Just as the disciples on that dusty road learned that they must depend on Christ for the fulfillment of the mission, we too must depend on Christ to continue building His church in the 21st century through people who place their faith in Him. The disciples did not understand the way in which He would build His church; nevertheless, they had to trust Him and depend on Him every step of the way.

The church today has its challenges as people approach it with a consumer mentality, that is, people view their church experience solely in terms of a product to be purchased or a service to be rendered. Has the consumer mentality influenced your understanding of the mission of the church?

Consumer mentality becomes visible when we make a list of what we are looking for in a church. Take worship, for example. Do you prefer exquisite music that reflects classical training and hours of practice? A full orchestra and a large choir that lifts your spirit and glorifies God certainly create a wonderful element of worship. Still, others describe their ideal worship as more contemporary and up-to-date with guitars and drums providing the accompaniment. This, too, can engage people in worship with great energy and meaning.

Maybe the music is not as important to you as the teaching. You want practical biblical answers to life's journey, and you want people to understand what you are going through, so you want to belong to a church where most of the people are in your season of life. Conversely, maybe you want to experience and learn from those older and younger than yourself, so you are looking for a multi-generational church.

Perhaps the most important thing for you is missions and evangelism. Does the church reach out to the poor and the needy? Are there opportunities to serve? Maybe the kind of programs offered for children and youth becomes the vanguard of your quest for the ideal church.

Many might not be able to put it into words, but they are looking for a church that feels a certain way. Hospitable? Passionate? Authentic? Mega-church? Small, intimate family-style? Trendy? Intense? What are you looking for? Many of these can be good elements in a church experience, yet none of them can have meaning outside the biblical mission of why the church exists. This begs the question, what should the church be? And, according to whom? You? Me?

The intrusion of consumerism into the church tears at the very fiber of what every church should aspire to be, which is to be healthy. When I talk with expectant parents, I often ask them, "Which do you want, a boy or a girl?" Many, if not all, will say, "We just want a healthy baby."

When my son Levi and his wife, Kelli, were expecting for the first time, Kelli suffered a miscarriage a couple of months into the pregnancy. It was a difficult, disappointing, and painful experience for them. Those of you who are grandparents can imagine Elli's and my elation upon receiving the news that they were expecting again. We all prayed for a full-term, healthy baby *boy* (well, I prayed for a boy). Even if you wrote out a list of attributes you would want for your child, one word would sum up all of those qualities: *healthy*.

So it is for the church. We should all desire to have healthy churches. Building people up to become healthy followers of Christ is more than a ministry philosophy. It is the primary reason for the church's existence. One of my good friends, Clancy Hayes, states that we are to "help people become complete and competent followers of Jesus Christ." I really like that phrase, but only healthy churches can accomplish this task.

I have a friend who served as lead pastor of a church that had suffered from discontent, several splits, and financial struggles. This church did not have a good reputation in the community, and the remaining members had almost given up hope that the church could recover.

On one particular Sunday morning, after many months of my friend's faithful ministry, the people responded with new hope that they could once again have an influence in their community. The church began to grow. Important things began to come together that would create momentum, which is something every pastor recognizes as a crucial component for growth. As my friend began to contemplate what the future held for his congregation, the big question that rumbled through his mind was no longer, "Can we survive?" Instead, it was, "How big can this church become?"

My friend shared with me that it was at this point that God showed up big in his heart. He said, "It was a whispered conversation I had with God that changed my life and ministry forever." God spoke, "You're asking the wrong questions about your church. Thus you're arriving at the wrong conclusion." My friend responded, "Then what is the right question?" God answered, "You should be asking questions of priority and purpose. Your question should be, 'What kind of people are we producing?'"

My friend has never been the same and neither have I. Too many times and in too many places, a pastor's work is measured by traditional criteria:

bodies, bucks and buildings. I have such a strong passion to move beyond maintenance mentality, where money and members pre-empt priority and purpose. Healthy churches make life transformation and spiritual maturity their top priority.

In this chapter, we will consider the mission of the church according to the Scriptures, as we scan five qualities of a healthy church. But, before we jump into the mission and the qualities, I want us to process four intentional questions. I was fortunate to be introduced to a study of Kennon L. Callahan's work in *Twelve Keys to an Effective Church*. Since then, the following questions have become a part of my thought when processing the mission of the church.

These questions are intended to help you in two ways. The first way is to encourage your reflection on the mission of the church. It is vital that you understand why the church exists, especially if you want your church experience to be free from consumer mentality. Secondly, these questions will help foster your own sense of direction as you partner with your local church. If you are a fully-devoted Christ-follower, God has designed you with a purpose. He has gifted you! He expects you to use your time, talents, and treasures to make a difference in your community. Scripture teaches us that He wants us to do this in partnership with a local church. We need to belong to a community of believers in order to maximize our efforts.

1. Where are we headed?

The first question confirms that we are to look forward. The wrong first question would be, "Where have we been?" That would only invite us to look at the past.

Our church courageously took the challenge this spring to read through the Bible in 90 days. One of the comments I overheard as people discussed reading through the Old Testament inspired me. They took note that God acted decisively and compassionately, powerfully and tenderly in the past. Then God moved on to the present and to the future. He led His people to His preferred future, the future He promised and prepared for them.

The church that looks to the future sees God. God goes before His church, inviting her to that which He has promised and prepared. This book is about enjoying the advantages of a life-giving relationship with Christ. We enjoy the advantages as we respond to His invitation. "Where are we headed?" confirms that we can take up this invitation.

2. What kind of future are we building?

Something far more important is at stake in developing an effective plan for the future than the simple survival of the local church. "What are we building?" addresses the lives and destinies of our families, our friends, and the many people whose lives will be changed by our efforts. I truly believe there is a direct correlation between the strength of the strongest church in a community and the character and quality of life in that community.

God invites us to a theology of service, not survival. He asks us to move beyond the maintenance and membership of our own existence to affect the lives and destinies of our families, the character and quality of life in our community, and the ministry of reconciliation in our world.

3. What are our strengths, gifts, and competencies?

If a local church denies its strengths, gifts, and competencies, it denies God. Jesus did not invite the disciples on that dirt road near the city of Caesarea Philippi to embrace a foolish optimism or a contemporary positive thinking strategy. He invited them to embrace a God-centered understanding of life. "I will build my church, and all the powers of hell will not conquer it. And I will give you the keys of the Kingdom of Heaven. Whatever you lock on earth will be locked in heaven, and whatever you open on earth will be opened in heaven" (Matthew 16:18-19, NLT).

There are too many churches suffering from low self-esteem who think more poorly of themselves than they should. We should not be guilty of denying God's ability to build His church through ordinary people who believe and depend on Him for the advancement of the local church.

I will never forget my first pastor/board retreat. I was serving as a senior pastor for the first time and was excited to lead the church into the future. The retreat was designed for us to break away for two days to strategize and begin our first attempt at long-range planning. I came prepared with enough newsprint to wallpaper the conference room twice. Before the first day was over, we had managed to list most of our problems, needs, concerns, weaknesses, and shortcomings.

I know I did not graduate first in my class, and I might have even missed the day long-range planning was discussed in Pastoral Leadership class, but I knew that day that something had gone awry. I was hoping we would have been energized by a dynamic plan to harvest lost people in our community. Instead, we harvested discouragement and despondency. Since that day, I have discovered that churches with excellent, experienced leadership do not focus on their shortcomings. They continue to do better what they do best.

I am not proposing that we deny or never examine our problems, needs, concerns, and shortcomings. By asking, "What are our strengths, gifts, and competencies?" we align ourselves with God's plan to build His church. A church that first claims its strengths is in a stronger position to then address its weaknesses.

4. What is God calling us to accomplish in mission?

I hope it is obvious that this question does not ask what we want to do. The question is not, "If we had a million dollars, what would we do?" Note that this question focuses on "we." It takes prayer, vision, and wisdom to discern the nature of God's mission. "What is God calling us to accomplish?" focuses us on intentional achievement, not on intricate activities. We are not given to the task of keeping people busily involved in church activities.

Please note the last word in the question, "mission." The church I serve raises large amounts of money annually for world missions, and it is a joy to partner with missionaries from around the world. I once heard a missionary introduce himself in a pastor's conference as a former missionary to Germany and currently a missionary in Washington.

God invites us to see that the day of mission is at hand. I recall Kennon Callahan, the author and church consultant I previously mentioned, sharing a story about a time he was working with a church. He writes:

> *Several of us were in the sanctuary, puzzling and praying as to what would best be helpful in advancing the future mission of that church. Their sanctuary has a remarkable stained glass window of Christ, standing at a door, knocking. The sunlight was coming through the window that day in an amazing way, and it dawned on me what that picture, what that image of Christ means in our time. In the churched culture of the 1950s, the understanding was that Christ stood at the door, knocking, hoping someone would come to the door and open the door and invite Christ **in** — to their lives.*

> *What that image means in our time, on one of the richest mission fields on the planet, is that Christ stands at the door, knocking, hoping someone will come to the door and open the door so that Christ can invite them **out** — to share his life in mission with the human hurts and hopes of people in our community. It is no longer a matter of us inviting Christ **in** — to our lives. It is now Christ inviting us **out** — to share his life — in mission."*[4] (emphasis added)

As I consider the church family over which God has given me charge, I feel the weightiness of getting it right — the accomplishment of His mission for us. I admit there are days when I struggle with other questions, just as my friend did. Questions like, "How big can we grow?" and, "Can we have impressive ministry and become the discussion of others?" I try to constantly keep before me these four intentional questions, which, again, are:

1. Where are we headed?
2. What kind of future are we building?
3. What are our strengths, gifts, and competencies?

4. What is God calling us to accomplish in mission?

These intentional questions have become particularly appropriate focal points in my prayer life. I invite you to make them focal points in your prayer life as well. They will help keep us from a consumer mentality regarding our church experience.

After being considered with significant thoughtfulness, these questions shift from intentional to invitational, personalized and designed to pull each one of us along in the path of partnership. If you are like me, you find yourself measuring where you are on this journey toward experiencing a healthy church and asking what are the key qualities in a healthy church.

Please allow me the liberty of presenting a fragment of biblical setting for the case of a healthy church. The apostle Paul helps us understand that each of us plays a vital role in the materialization of a healthy church.

> 11 *He is the one who gave these gifts to the church: the apostles, the prophets, the evangelists, and the pastors and teachers.* 12 *Their responsibility is to equip God's people*

to do his work and build up the church, the body of Christ, 13 until we come to such unity in our faith and knowledge of God's Son that we will be mature and full grown in the Lord, measuring up to the full stature of Christ.

14 Then we will no longer be like children, forever changing our minds about what we believe because someone has told us something different or because someone has cleverly lied to us and made the lie sound like the truth.

15 Instead, we will hold to the truth in love, becoming more and more in every way like Christ, who is the head of his body, the church. 16 Under his direction, the whole body is fitted together perfectly. As each part does its own special work, it helps the other parts grow, so that the whole body is healthy and growing and full of love (Ephesians 4:11-16, NLT).

Paul pens a considerable phrase, "As each part does its own special work . . ." The pastor has a significant part in the work of the church. It is central to understand that the pastor's mandate is to equip and empower people in the journey of personal maturity and public ministry, but every member has an equally significant part in his own way. When this is a reality within a local church, Paul states, the whole body is healthy, growing, and experiencing authentic care.

Still, some people have erroneous ideas about ministry. They entertain the incompatible concepts that the pastor alone can do important spiritual work, while the Scriptures teach the priesthood of all believers. They correctly believe that God values the ministry of all believers by gifting them to contribute in ministry, yet they categorize "holy" ministries for the professional minister and leave the mediocre chores for themselves.

Take the common occurrence of hospital visitation. Visiting the sick is a ministry given to the entire community of believers. The Bible gives no indication or support that this is solely a pastor's responsibility. Even though lay ministers visit the sick, counsel the bereaved, or intervene during a crisis, many expect the pastor to duplicate the task. When 12 people visit someone in the hospital, but the pastor does not visit, will the patient complain that he or she has not been visited? If so, the implication is that only the pastor's ministry is meaningful, and the layperson's ministry or time is insufficient or insignificant. That, friend, is unhealthy because it is unbiblical.

Christ is the head of the church and under His direction, we, the people, fit together perfectly. Eugene Peterson states that Christ keeps us in step with one another (Ephesians 4:16, MSG).

Have you ever put your face above a headless frame painted to represent something, such as a muscle man or a woman in a red and white polka dotted bathing suit? Do you remember how ridiculous that looked because your head did not match the rest of the body? If we could picture Christ as the head and then us as the body, individually at first, then as a community, and then as the church worldwide, would the world laugh at the misfit? Or, on the other hand, would they be amazed at the human body being so closely related to the divine head?

A healthy church is a community of people who increasingly reflect Christ as He is revealed through the Scriptures. I long to experience true health and authenticity in the local church. I think Freya Stark stated it quite well when she said, "There can be no happiness if the things we believe in are different from the things we do."[5]

As we look at the following five qualities of a healthy church, consider how you can help make this a reality in your local fellowship. My goal is to help you move forward with a sense of urgency and ownership, in order that you fuse what you believe to what you experience in real life. These qualities do not cover everything that can be said about the church, nor may they be the qualities that are most important. Certainly the ordinances of baptism and communion, as well as significant prayer ministries, are essentials in a biblical church, and yet they are not discussed here. I have chosen to highlight these five qualities because they are repeatedly discovered, in some fashion, among healthy churches. In contrast, nearly every church practices at least the ordinances, even churches that are anemic.

1. A Clear and Concise, God-Inspired Vision

I so appreciate the manner in which Eugene Peterson restated Proverbs 29:18 in *The Message*: *If people can't see what God is doing, they stumble all over themselves; but when they attend to what he reveals, they are most blessed.*

Vision acts as an anchor to hold the church steady, strong, and secure. Sadly, too many churches function without a clear understanding of why they exist. They have no vision of what God wants them to do; consequently, they stumble all over themselves.

Conversely, a healthy church is clear and concise in its purpose. The local fellowship that shares God-given vision and gifts is strengthened and united in purpose, faith, and love. When a group of Christ-followers understands and embraces a unified vision, their energy, creativity, and resources are focused on the goal. Health becomes a reality when a clear, concise vision is embraced, because the common experience bonds them together and creates a shared identity. This produces a strong loyalty to the vision and to each other.

Additionally, a clear, concise, God-inspired vision energizes the church to persevere through difficult or challenging times and enables believers to rise above their individuality in order to move forward together to reach a lost and dying world.

Let me encourage you to assist your pastoral team in the fulfillment of your church's vision. Embrace it wholeheartedly. Pray for the fulfillment of the vision. Seek God to identify your role in reaching the vision. Help new people learn the vision.

In the Appendix, you will find the Mission, Vision, and Values of First Assembly.

2. A Strong, Effective Leadership Team

Second, a healthy church develops and maintains a strong, effective leadership team. When I say "effective team," I mean a winning team. For any team to be a winning team, they must create a winning mentality and climate. Part of a winning climate is choosing the right people for key roles. These individuals will then weld together relationally in both form and function. The pastor can never and should never be the whole "show" in a church. Healthy churches do not spotlight individual leaders; rather, they highlight team-based ministry developed by strong leadership.

Think back with me to the 1992 NCAA championship game between the Michigan Wolverines and the Duke Blue Devils. The Wolverines were poised to put an end to Duke's back-to-back dreams. They were gifted, entertaining trend-busters. The "Fab Five," we called them — one up on the Beatles. Chris Webber, Jalen Rose, Juwan Howard, Jimmy King, and Ray Jackson were lean, teen, University of Michigan models of baggy fashion, playing basketball in droopy shorts that became a global style. Without a doubt, they were considered the most talented five freshmen ever recruited to play Big Ten basketball. They were heralded as the best of the best, and a string of conference championships seemed inevitable. Wolverine fans around the country eagerly anticipated a national championship. Although the "Fab Five" accomplished some incredible things, they never won a national championship, losing to Duke 71 to 51. Despite their talent and the advantage of playing for the University of Michigan, the "Fab Five" never realized their potential. For some reason, they were not able to forge their talents, focus their energies, and fulfill their most important goal.

    Some church staffs are like the "Fab Five." God has given them the gifts and poured out His blessings, but they fail to realize their potential. They go about ministry like independent contractors, negotiating over resources, rooms, and volunteers. They spend more time navigating around schedules and calendars than collaborating. When I realize what is at stake, conviction captures my heart, for we are not simply moving a basketball up and down a wooden court. We are called to carry out God's mission, nothing less than the redemption of the world.

    How can I help to promote strong leadership in my church?

- Pray for the lead pastor and anyone else involved in the hiring process of both

the pastoral and support teams.
- Volunteer in a ministry in your local church. Be conscientious and do everything you can to complete assignments and projects with the highest standard of excellence.
- Pray daily for all the ministry teams in your church.

3. Experience a Healthy, Balanced Pace

Strong, healthy churches maintain a healthy pace and balance in all of their ministries. Too often, church leaders and volunteers can become burned out if they get out of biblical balance. On an individual level, a biblical balance places God as your top priority. Committing to a growing relationship with Christ is the beginning of balancing your life. Family is your first ministry responsibility, and then you seek to discover other ministry opportunities as God leads. It is unrealistic to believe that if your time spent developing a growing relationship with God is squeezed out, you will be able to balance the other two in a God-honoring fashion.

Balance in the church is just as delicate. Sometimes we go to extremes in one direction or another. Rick Warren developed this thought comprehensively in his book, *The Purpose Driven Church*, so I will not go into depth on the subject here. Just note that God designed the church to be in perfect balance with His purpose. For example, if the church emphasizes evangelism over fellowship, community care will be deficient. Highlight fellowship over outreach, and the church will become too inward-focused. Another form of subtle imbalance is gaining head knowledge to the lapse of living the application of the Good News in the marketplace.

How can I demonstrate a God-honoring balance in my life, and subsequently in my church experience?

- Get enough rest.
- Guard your time in order to develop your relationship with God and your family.
- Respect your pastor's time for rest.
- Practice what you learn throughout the week and throughout your lifetime.

4. Intentionally and Relevantly Reaching the Un-churched

Today we are faced with incredible opportunities to reach out to the world around us.

Yet anyone who has a desire to be used by God in our emerging culture needs to develop three fundamental skills:

1. We need to build a compassionate church that will communicate authentic community to a broken society.
2. We need to read the Bible, reminding ourselves of the vision of God's Kingdom on earth and the values of a covenant relationship given by God's grace.
3. We need to study our culture, for it is in seeing what is happening in our culture that we discover the best way to communicate the message of the Gospel. This is not a new idea. In Acts 17, the apostle Paul was a careful observer of the culture of Athens as he prepared to speak to the Athenian people. The application of Paul's model requires that we look carefully at the world we live in — the hopes, fears, and longings of our emerging culture.

The message of the Gospel is forever relevant, but in an ever-changing culture, it is important that we communicate this message in an accessible way.

As we learn to become careful observers of the world around us, we will discover the open doors within our culture that present us with an opportunity to share how Jesus can transform a life. As people who want to be used by God in this emerging culture, we also need to be careful observers of our own lives to ensure that we are authentically living the message we are trying to convey.

During World War II, some American soldiers took the body of their buddy to a local cemetery. The priest stopped them, saying, "You can't bury your friend here if he is not a Catholic." Discouraged but not defeated, the boys buried their fellow soldier just outside the cemetery fence. When they came to pay their respects the next morning, they could not find the grave. They questioned the priest about it, and he said, "The first part of the night I stayed awake, disturbed by what I had told you. The second part of the night, I spent moving the fence."

The church in every generation has the responsibility to preach the Gospel, win the lost, train the disciples, heal the broken-hearted, and lift up those who are fallen. That function has been given to no one except the church. Healthy churches understand this. The message that pulsates throughout the New Testament, the incredible challenge that comes again to the church in every generation, is that the church is the mind through which Christ thinks, the heart through which Christ loves, the voice through which Christ speaks, the hands through which Christ helps, and the body of believers through whom Christ works.

What is my role in reaching the un-churched?
- Recognize that you are a part of the Great Commission — you do not just pay the pastoral team to evangelize.
- Open your eyes and carefully observe the world around you so you can learn to more effectively share the message of the Gospel that lives in your heart.
- Balance your life between connections with those who are lost and those who are already found.

5. Disciple People in Growth Environments — Mid-Size and Small Groups

Have you ever wondered how God transforms people? Transformation occurs as we recognize that God created us to live in an interactive relationship with the Trinity. Our task is not to transform ourselves but to stay connected with God in as many aspects of our lives as possible. As we pay attention to the nudges of the Holy Spirit, we become fully-developed followers of Christ. Our task is to do the connecting, while God does the perfecting.

The spiritual exercise of connecting to God is linked to the spiritual practice of community. Sadly, this spiritual practice is misunderstood in many churches. Many envision community as people standing around a campfire holding hands and singing or having coffee and a donut between the worship service and the Sunday school hour. While there may be moments of warm feelings and pleasant conversation, community as a growth environment is intentional.

Transformation involves growth, and growth requires an environment for growing. "Environment" implies a condition that surrounds; it speaks to the totality of circumstances and conditions that affect and influence the growth of something or someone. Jesus created an environment in which His church would grow by forming a group, a community. When you consider that Jesus had three short years to set the plan of salvation in motion, it is remarkable that He invested so much time hanging out with an entourage of simple men and women. By this choice, He prioritized the centrality of community.

Because of who God is, there is no such thing as private or individual Christianity. Consequently, true transformation cannot ensue outside growth environments. Michael E. Williams puts it this way in *The Storyteller's Companion to the Bible*: "The spiritual discipline of hospitality is a continual process of transforming sojourners into kinfolk and strangers into friends."

Unhealthy churches do not have positive environments for people to grow as fully-developed followers of Christ. Conversely, the early church did experience community that created a warm, nurturing environment where people felt accepted and safe. I would like to think they got beyond the social hour with coffee and donuts and began to move toward sincere conversations about life.

Scripture indicates sincere conversations about life within the context of a growth environment are a priority. The Apostle Paul instructed Titus to establish growth environments by helping the older men to live wisely and respectfully and to demonstrate a strong faith in a loving manner. Older women were to live appropriately as well. Why? So they could speak into the lives of others (Titus 2:2-7).

Robert Mulholland, in his book, *Invitation To A Journey: A Road Map for Spiritual Formation*, acknowledged, "Others become agents of grace in our growth toward wholeness in Christ while we become agents of God's grace in their growth." In essence, he defines spiritual formation as the process of being conformed to the image of Christ for the sake of others. Wow! This is a powerful combination. Can you imagine the health of that kind of environment? When personal spiritual formation for the sake of others becomes a reality, positive environments result.

Given that the early church practiced the priority of community as growth environments, God considered them worthy of greater stewardship and added to their number (Acts 2:47). The Apostle Paul later taught, "My job was to plant the seed in your hearts, and Apollos watered it, but it was God, not we, who made it grow" (1 Corinthians 3:6, NLT).

What does growth look like? A healthy church will grow, so when you open the door and look into the life of a healthy church, the growth of its people shows up in various ways. Here are just a few:

- An expanding number of people are involved in missional outreach, both at home and abroad.
- Older members sense a fresh call of responsibility for the following

generation's success by mentoring and encouraging them.
- Younger people express an appreciation for older members and attend events to learn from and minister to them as well.
- An increase in prayer for the lost and ministry opportunities.
- Hospitality and acceptance of new people, regardless of their spiritual condition.
- Increased sacrificial giving.
- Increased fruit and ministry of the Holy Spirit.
- An expanding number of people experiencing community within small groups.
- Husbands and wives fulfilling their biblical roles and experiencing healthy marriages.
- Young boys and girls navigating the critical transitions from elementary school to middle school to high school through college and on to the marketplace as healthy Christ-followers.
- A corporate enthusiasm for connecting

with God and each other through the weekend services.

How can I be intentional in helping my church enjoy the blessing of growth environments?
- Commit to growing in maturity through a small group journey.
- Process the attitudes of love that are important in expressing whether community is to flourish and discuss them with someone (I Corinthians 13:4-7).
- Recognize that I have value to others, whether or not I feel useful to them.
- When attending a weekend service, notice the people around me. Pause and say a prayer of thanks for them.
- Practice the gift of hospitality. Take a risk and connect relationally with others by serving together.

Are you willing to help your local fellowship become an intentionally healthy environment? If so, mobilize the full employment of your fellowship to uphold a clear vision, begin to value well-balanced ministry, support and encourage your leadership team to take risks and make courageous decisions to reach the un-churched, and cultivate growth environments. You will not be disappointed. As we grow healthier, we develop into people who can build others up, and our church becomes a place of true community, submitting to God's plan.

It is my hope that through this book you will move forward with confidence, enjoying the advantages of a life-giving relationship with Christ. I trust you have caught sight of Jesus inviting the tired, fearful, and hurting to *come to Him*. My prayer is that you discovered Jesus encouraging you toward maturity, having the faith and courage to *ask Him* for clear vision. In addition, I pray that you embrace Jesus as He offers friendship that includes security, influence, and belonging as you *remain in Him*. Now, you will irresistibly appreciate Jesus pronouncing that He will build His church with ordinary people who *depend on Him* to bless those who believe.

6 The Greatest News of All Time

> The doctrine of redemption is founded on a mere pecuniary idea corresponding to that of a debt, which another person might pay . . .
> Thomas Paine, *The Age of Reason*

> He paid a debt he did not owe,
> I owed a debt I could not pay.
> I needed someone to wash my sins away.
> And now I sing a brand new song,
> "Amazing Grace" all day long,
> Christ Jesus paid a debt that I could never pay.
> Anonymous

Congratulations, you have made it this far in the book. On the other hand, maybe you just turned to the back of the book to see how it ends. Nonetheless, in all reality, this chapter may represent the beginning of the journey for some of you. You might need to know something about God that has not been related to you in detail.

No matter how you feel about yourself or how others treat you, God loves you and longs to be in a life-giving relationship with you. His love is constant. The whole story of the Bible is a story of God's love for you. "But you, O God, are both tender and kind, not easily angered, immense in love, and you never, never quit" (Psalm 86:15, MSG).

The worst news imaginable.

All of us human beings are born with a broken relationship with God. Because of sin, we are all separated from the God who loves us. Sin is the word the Bible uses to describe anything we do that is inconsistent with God's plan for our lives. His plan is perfect, because He is perfectly pure (holy). Therefore, He cannot ignore sin, and we are condemned to death because of our sin. He cannot just look the other way. God still loves us, but our sin damages our relationship by driving a wedge between us and Him.

In a letter to people in Rome, the Apostle Paul declared that sin is very costly. He said it this way, "For the wages of sin is death . . ." (Romans 6:23). Sin demands payment, and this death sentence hangs over us. I know that sounds harsh and seems overwhelmingly disturbing until you realize that God did something so you could experience a restored relationship with Him.

The best news ever.

What God did is remarkable. It is the greatest news of all time! He paid our debt of sin by sending His only Son, Jesus, to earth as a man. We celebrate the gift of Jesus on Christmas. Jesus was God in a human body. He lived a real life experiencing all that we do, yet He never sinned. He was consistent with God's plan.

According to God's plan, Jesus was accused of crimes He did not commit and was condemned to death. Even in this, Jesus acted intentionally within God's plan. He died by an act of His own will. "No one can take my life from me. I lay down my life voluntarily" (John 10:18, NLT).

The Gospel is called the Good News because we are offered a pardon for all the wrong we have ever done and will ever do. We can experience a restored relationship with God through the work of Christ.

This is how the Bible describes what was done for us on the cross:

> . . . *God has now made [you] to share in the very life of Christ! He has forgiven you all your sins: Christ has utterly wiped out the damning evidence of broken laws and commandments which always hung over our heads, and has completely annulled it by nailing it over his own head on the cross* (Colossians 2:14, Phillips NT).

Jesus Christ came to earth, lived a perfect life, and died on the cross for my sin and for yours. It has all been paid for — every sin you have ever committed or have yet to commit. The ones you have not even thought about — next week, next year, 10 years from now — have already been paid for.

When Jesus Christ died on the cross, He stretched out His hands and said, "It is finished" (John 19:30). He did not say, "I am finished" because He wasn't. It was not about that; He came to life three days later (John 20). He was not finished, but the payment for all of your sins, the plan of salvation, was finished (complete).

In the Greek language, "It is finished" is actually one word, *tetelestai*, meaning "paid in full." When a person paid off a bill, they would stamp *tetelestai* on it. That meant it was paid in full. How long do you remember a bill you have paid? You forget it. Or, when a person served his time in prison and the sentence was commuted, the prison papers were stamped with *tetelestai* — paid in full. You are a free man. You can go. You are not in prison any more.

When Jesus said on the cross, "It is finished," He was saying, "*Tetelestai!* Paid in full. I have paid for all the things you have ever done wrong so you can experience a restored relationship with God and have the security of eternal life in heaven."

The Bible explains it this way:

> 4 Even before the world was made, God had already chosen us to be his through our union with Christ, so that we would be holy and without fault before him. Because of his love 5 God had already decided that through Jesus Christ he would make us his children— this was his pleasure and purpose.

6 *Let us praise God for his glorious grace, for the free gift he gave us in his dear Son! 7 For by the blood of Christ we are set free, that is, our sins are forgiven. How great is the grace of God, 8 which he gave to us in such large measure!* (Ephesians 1:4-8, TEV).

Jesus suffered a brutal death so that we would not have to pay the price for our sin. His death was payment. He sacrificed Himself on the cross in our place. His death became ours. If we accept God's gift of grace, which many have said means **G**race **R**eceived **A**t **C**hrist's **E**xpense, we begin a life-giving relationship with God through Jesus Christ.

Think about this. If there had been any other way for your sins to be forgiven or for you to get to heaven besides Jesus Christ dying on the cross, don't you think God would have used it rather than let His Son go through all that suffering?

The fact is, friend, <u>there is no other way</u>! If there were, Jesus Christ's death was a waste. The only chance you have to experience a restored relationship with Him is to accept the free forgiveness of Jesus Christ, who paid for your sins on the cross. If you have not accepted that free gift, please consider doing so right now. Do not waste another second of your life.

How can a person experience this restored relationship?

The Bible makes it clear that this restored relationship is a free gift; it cannot be earned or won by good works or generous behavior. Salvation can be received only by faith in Christ. The first step of faith is to pray and ask Jesus to forgive you and to accept Him as the leader of your life. This step includes admitting that you have sinned and are sorry for those sins. Then, ask God to help you follow Christ as you live a new and changed life that is consistent with His purpose for you.

You can express this prayer in your own words, or you can use the following prayer:

> Dear God, I need you to take control of my life. I need you more than I have ever known. I admit my sin. I have not lived a life that is consistent with your plan for my life, and that has resulted in my living under the penalty of a death sentence. I believe you sent your Son, Jesus, to show me your love and to pay the price for my sin by dying in my place. Thank you, Jesus, for your sacrifice on the cross. Forgive me, come into my life, and help me to follow your purpose for my

life. I choose to follow you the rest of my life. Thank you for the gift of eternal life. I receive this gift by faith in Jesus Christ. Amen!

If you have repeated this prayer and meant it in your heart, you can be confident that you have a restored relationship with God and that all your sins have been forgiven. "But if we confess our sins to him, he is faithful and just to forgive us and to cleanse us from every wrong" (1 John 1:9, NLT).

> 9 *For if you confess with your mouth that Jesus is Lord and believe in your heart that God raised him from the dead, you will be saved.* 10 *For it is by believing in your heart that you are made right with God, and it is by confessing with your mouth that you are saved.* 11 *As the Scriptures tell us, "Anyone who believes in him will not be disappointed"* (Romans 10:9-11, NLT).

Date I gave my life to Christ: _____

I told: _____

Church I will attend: _____

Appendix — Our Focus & Mission

Our Mission: First Assembly exists to fulfill the Great Commission, as a healthy, visible, and growing community of Christ-followers, experiencing and leading others into an authentic Spirit-filled life.

Our Vision: We envision a Spirit-filled environment that emphasizes relationships, relevant ministry, spiritual growth, celebration, and generosity.

Our Initiatives: God desires for each of us to experience a process of continual growth and transformation into the likeness of Jesus. We strive toward our aim of growing healthy, visible, authentic Spirit-filled Christ-followers through the following six initiatives:

EXPRESS JESUS TO OUR WORLD (Sharing/Evangelism)

Definition: To communicate and live out the transformational reality of the abundant life God offers all people.

Reach the un-churched people of central Iowa with the life-changing message of Jesus Christ, by building strategic bridges between our church and the community as we show the love of Christ to those we serve. We value using culturally relevant methods that cause people to recognize their need for God and motivate them to draw near to Him. We recognize that the Holy Spirit is the agent of change and that our responsibility is to intentionally convey the message of Christ and create an environment in which the Holy Spirit can work to transform human hearts.

2 Corinthians 5:20 (Phillips NT) *We are now Christ's ambassadors, as though God were appealing direct to you through us. As his personal representatives we say, "Make your peace with God." For God caused Christ, who himself knew nothing of sin, actually to be sin for our sakes, so that in Christ we might be made good with the goodness of God.*

ENCOUNTER GOD (Celebrating God's Presence — Worshipping)

Definition: A point at which we interface with the transformational power of God, which leads to life and freedom.

The Christian faith-walk is all about encountering God . . . it's how a relationship of love with Him grows. While an encounter with God cannot be manufactured, certain environments (primary environment — weekend services) can make an encounter more likely to happen. Worship is glorifying God and enjoying His presence with all of one's heart, soul, mind, and strength. Therefore, we stress the core belief that God is spirit and those who worship Him must worship in spirit and truth. We strive to practice personal and corporate worship through song, the teaching of God's Word, and faith-filled prayer ministry.

Psalm 9:1-2 (NLT) 1 *I will thank you, LORD, with all my heart; I will tell of all the marvelous things you have done. 2 I will be filled with joy because of you. I will sing praises to your name, O Most High.*

ENGAGE WITH ONE ANOTHER (Belonging)

Definition: To build relationships with other people and live the life God gives in community.

Doing life together is what community is all about. When people relate to one another on a personal level, a more responsive environment for care and shared spiritual growth is created. This is not about church "activities" — it's about getting to know people on a deeper, caring level and building the type of relationships that a small group fosters so well. This involvement encompasses acts that inspire hope, instill confidence, lift spirits, and provide needed support in a way that fosters a sense of genuine care and belonging. We strive to exemplify God's love for humanity modeled by

Jesus himself and commanded for the Church of the New Testament to follow in order to care for God's family.

Acts 2:42-44 (NIV) *42 They devoted themselves to the apostles' teaching and to the fellowship, to the breaking of bread and to prayer. 43 Everyone was filled with awe, and many wonders and miraculous signs were done by the apostles. 44 All the believers were together and had everything in common.*

ENCOURAGE MATURITY (Growing)

Definition: Doing the right thing at the right time for the right reason at the right degree.

Teaching God's people to grow to full devotion to Christ through appropriate biblical teaching, the development of tools and resources for growth, authentic community, and the practice of personal spiritual disciplines such as prayer, worship, Bible study, journaling, giving, service, fasting, etc. We seek to provide appropriate biblical teaching for all ages and for all levels of spiritual maturity using a variety of settings, such as Small Groups, formal classrooms, one-on-one teaching and mentoring relationships.

Hebrews 6:1 (NIV) *Therefore let us leave the elementary teachings about Christ and go on to maturity . . .*

EQUIPPED FOR MINISTRY (Serving)

Definition: Every believer will discover their purpose, passion, and place in ministry.

Serving, or extension, is actively demonstrating God's love through the use of our unique individual passions, spiritual gifts, personal style, and resources to meet the needs of the body of Christ and the world. We understand that all of our resources, including time, talents and treasures belong to God, and use of these resources should be guided by spiritual priorities.

1 Peter 4:10 (NLT) *God has given gifts to each of you from his great variety of spiritual gifts. Manage them well so that God's generosity can flow through you.*

EXCELLENCE IN MINISTRY and LIFE (Synergizing)

Definition: Every pastor, support person, and volunteer developing personally and professionally, resulting in an effective and efficient team.

We stress the importance of creating and maintaining grace-filled environments that increase personal and professional effectiveness and competencies.

Colossians 3:17 (NLT) *And whatever you do or say, let it be as a representative of the Lord Jesus, all the while giving thanks through him to God the Father.*

Our Strategy: Three-Step Strategy for Spiritual Growth

How Do We Develop People as Authentic Spirit-filled Followers of Christ?

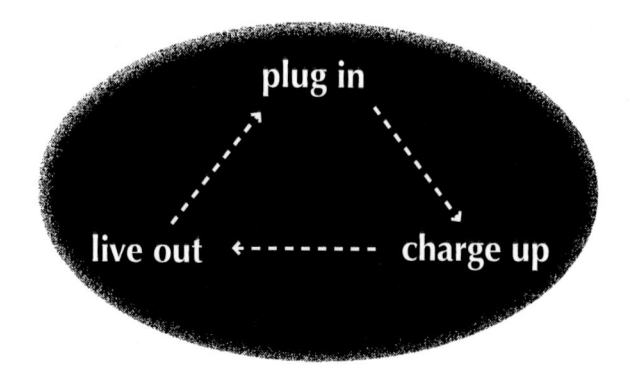

plug in

live out ← - - - - - - charge up

In Acts 2:42–47, we see a snapshot of what the church should be experiencing. Essentially, we see a community of people **loving God, one another, and their world.** Like an equilateral triangle, where all three sides must be the same size, the early church recognized the equal importance of all three of these relationships.

In fact, these three types of relationships interact so much that it is impossible to differentiate one from another. We show our love for God in our love for others and we cannot love the world if we are not living in a healthy relationship with God and His people.

So the question is: How do we live out this example in the 21st century with the constant barrage of information, activities, and interruptions? At First Assembly, we encourage people to do three things . . . **Plug In, Charge Up, and Live Out**.

PLUG IN . . . by making a connection with God and people at our weekend services. The connection makes significant spiritual formation in your life possible. Our weekend services are full of opportunities to worship, serve, and receive God's instruction to enjoy a life-giving relationship with Christ. A plugged-in person is on his/her way to being a stronger, healthier and joy-filled person. On the weekend, age-based ministries reach and equip children, students, young adults and aged adults to become healthy, visible followers of Christ as well.

CHARGE UP . . . to become more like Christ in *small group* gatherings. Small groups are an essential part of our culture. In relation to our mission to *fulfill the Great Commission as healthy, visible, and authentic followers of Christ*, they provide a major avenue for living out these original pursuits that Christ gives us as His followers (Matthew 22:37-39). Our most common type of small group follows a "sermon-based" format. In these groups, members meet to discuss and ask questions about the weekend message. As they talk through the lesson, participants find ways to personally and practically encourage each other to apply the Bible to their lives.

We have small groups that focus on many other interests and needs as well, with the intention of building authentic friendships and fostering spiritual growth in or towards Christ.

At First Assembly, there are two primary types of groups to deepen our understanding of God's Word and apply His teachings to our lives.

> Small Groups — mid-week, home-based groups of 8-12 people who discuss the Sunday message and accompanying Scriptures.
>
> Mid-Size Groups (ABC's) — a semester-based system offering classes covering everything from basic theology to practical tools for living as a Christ-follower.

LIVE OUT . . . your faith by serving at First Assembly or in your local community. Jesus modeled living out the realities of a life-giving relationship with God for us. He served the people around Him, and the people benefited because of His involvement in their lives. First Assembly has partnered with many ministries and missionaries, and the opportunities to live out your faith are numerous and various. Living out your faith demonstrates the authenticity of your relationship with Christ.

Our Accountability: Key Questions That Keep Us on Target

Spiritual Transformation

Life change occurs as we experience God's grace through understanding the Bible, which we believe to be God's Word, engage in meaningful worship, and practice prayer and spiritual disciplines.

> Are you growing in the Bible, worship and prayer?

One-Life Relationships

Everyone knows at least one person (one-life) who has not

experienced God's grace and love. We value praying for that individual regularly, living an authentic faith before them, and having intentional spiritual conversations in the course of everyday life.

> Who is your one-life relationship?

Authentic Community

God's dream is for people to experience community with Him and with one another. Authentic community happens when people come together in love, acceptance, and encouragement. Community and life change happen best in small groups.

> Are you in a small group?

Generous Giving

Everything we are and have is anchored in God's generosity in our lives. Practicing wise stewardship of our lives and giving back financially is a direct response to His generous nature toward us.

> Are you living generously toward God?

Intentional Serving

We demonstrate God's love through the use of our spiritual gifts, talents, and personalities in support of our collective strategy to meet the needs of others who may or may not know Him.

> Where are you serving?

Expressed Compassion and Care

Expressing care and love toward others shows our love toward God. We value acts of compassion and kindness to all people, including the poor, the under-resourced, and the hurting in our society.

> Are you expressing love to others?

Guiding Values:

1. Spirit-led ministry — prayer is key.
2. Biblically measured — simplicity — staying centered on Christ and His Word.
3. Teamwork — we value each person's gifts and participation.
4. Relationships — pursuing and developing authentic, healthy relationships — healthy marriages and families.

5. Strong and intentional discipleship journey — full devotion — wholehearted Christians.
6. Evangelistically bold and creative.
7. Socially relevant and responsible.
8. Excellence in ministry and life — doing our best for God.
9. Fun — we enjoy following Jesus.
10. Healthy pace of life.

Endnotes

Chapter One: He Knows

1. John Maxwell, *Today Matters: 12 Daily Practices to Guarantee Tomorrow's Success* (New York: Warner Faith, 2004), 19-20.
2. Hodge, *Systematic Theology I*, 440-441.

Chapter Two: Come To Me

1. John Bacon, "Guess Who's Not Coming to a Bush Dinner," *USA Today*, 5 June 2002, 3A; from staff and wire reports.
2. Fred W. Kiger, "Namath was as good as his word." Retrieved December 6, 2007, from http://espn.go.com/classic/s/add_Namath_Joe.html
3. John Ortberg, *The Life You've Always Wanted* (Grand Rapids, Michigan: Zondervan, 1997), 83.
4. Adapted from "The Moped vs The Ferrari." Retrieved December 12, 2007, from http://www.buildeazy.com/joke_page_3.html
5. Rob Stein, "Laughter's Link to Health May Be in the Blood." Retrieved February 6, 2008, from www.washingtonpost.com/wp-dyn/articles/A31927-2005Mar13.html
6. Excerpt from *The Fellowship of the Ring* by J.R.R. Tolkien, Copyright © 1954, 1965 by J.R.R. Tolkien. Copyright © renewed 1982 by Christopher R. Tolkien, Michael H.R. Tolkien, John F.R. Tolkien, and Priscilla M.A.R. Tolkien. Copyright © renewed 1993 by

Christopher R. Tolkien, Michael H.R. Tolkien, John F.R. Tolkien, and Priscilla M.A.R. Tolkien.

Chapter Three: Ask Me

1. John M. Dresher, "Empty chair," *Pulpit Digest*, May/June 1981, 39.

2. John 10:10 adapted from *The Message*.

3. May Wong, Retrieved September 7, 2007, from www.news.yahoo.com

4. The most famous hierarchy of human drives was put forward by Abraham Maslow, working from the base of physiological needs to what he termed "self-actualization." I am unsure of its original source. It was first suggested to my thinking by Rick Warren's use of it in "The Purpose Driven Preaching Conference," delivered at Saddleback Valley Community Church, Lake Forest, California, 1999.

5. R. Kent Hughes, *Mark, Volume 2: Jesus, Servant and Savior* (Westchester, Illinois: Crossway Books, 1989), 74.

6. *Joe vs. the Volcano* (Amblin Entertainment/Warner Brothers, 1990), directed by John Patrick Shanley.

Chapter Four: Remain in Me

1. James A. Michener, *The Source* (New York: Macmillan, 1978), 148.

2. Charles R. Swindoll, *The Grace Awakening* (Dallas: Word Publishing, 1990), 6.

3. C.S. Lewis, *The Voyage of the Dawn Treader* (London: Collins, 1974), 102.

4. Pruning. (n.d.). *Columbia Electronic Encyclopedia*. Retrieved February 7, 2008, from Reference.com website: http://www.reference.com/browse/columbia/pruning

5. "Milestones," *Time* (4-23-07), 22; "Paralyzed NFL player Stingley dies at 55," Associated Press, www.sportingnews.com (4-5-07); Peter Smith, "Darryl Stingley and forgiveness," www.courier-journal.com (4-9-07).

6. Brian Lowery, associate editor, PreachingToday.com; source: Jonathan Petre, "Church invites could boost congregations," www.telegraph.co.uk (5-4-07).

7. Thom S. Rainer and Sam S. Rainer III, "Getting to Know Today's Unchurched" from *Outreach Magazine*, May/June 2007. Retrieved February 9, 2008, from http://www.christianitytoday.com/outreach/articles/todaysunchurched.html

8. Brian L. Harbour, *Rising Above the Crowd* (Nashville: Broadman Press, 1988), 68-69.

9. Byrd Baggett, *The Soul of Winning* (Successories Library, 2001), 21.

Chapter Five: Depend on Me

1. "About Yogi," Retrieved February 18, 2008, from http://www.yogiberra.com/about.html

2. Loren B. Mead, *The Once and Future Church* (Washington, D.C.: The Alban Institute, 1994), 28.

Endnotes

3. J. W. McGarvey, *The New Testament Commentary: Vol. I - Matthew and Mark*. Database © 2007 WORDsearch Corp.

4. Kennon L. Callahan, *Twelve Keys to an Effective Church, The Leaders' Guide* (San Francisco: Harper & Row, 1983), 43.

5. In 1928, at age 35, Freya Stark established herself at the forefront of exploration with an audacious journey into forbidden territory of the Syrian Druze. While there, she was thrown into a military prison, but not before she had trekked across the infamous Valley of the Assassins occupied by a heretical sect of Muslims known for committing political and religious murders.